My American Dream

How Great Teachers Inspired My Life

Sylvia Rimm, Ph.D.

Gifted
UNLIMITED

Edited by: Frances Irene Regan
Interior design: The Printed Page
Cover design: The Printed Page

Published by
Gifted Unlimited, LLC
12340 U.S. Highway 42, No. 453
Goshen, KY 40026
www.giftedunlimitedllc.com

ISBN: 978-1-953360-45-8

Acknowledgements

As a child of immigrants to this country I have so many people to acknowledge for their contributions to the story of my exciting lifetime.

First, I must acknowledge my father's cousin, Mrs. Rose Pargot, for sponsoring my parents' immigration to the United States. Secondly, I am so thankful to my loving parents, Harry and Reva Barkan, for their messages of the importance of hard work and their emphasis on family togetherness. Also, special thanks to my older sisters and their spouses, Vivian and Irving and Frances and Harvey and their children, or our cousins by the dozens, for all their family support.

My most sincere and extreme thanks go to all my teachers from kindergarten through the universities. In kindergarten, Miss Moore wanted me to skip a grade, and in 4th grade, Miss Shoobridge gave Joan and me some extra hard work because she saw that we were gifted and thus encouraged our excitement and love of learning. There were many more teachers who inspired me along the way. Mrs. Herbert, my guidance counselor, made a huge and significant contribution to my life by making it possible for me to go to college and explaining how I might earn the scholarships I needed to enroll—something I had never expected I could do.

I met my husband, Alfred, in college, and we inspired each other to continue our education to earn doctorate degrees. He encouraged me at a time when women rarely went to graduate school. My college professors continued to inspire me. In turn, we encouraged our four children to acquire doctorate degrees so they, too, could make their small contributions to our world.

It is because I so appreciated my learning from so many teachers at every level that I wished to address the impact that teachers can make on immigrant students to assist them in understanding the amazing opportunities that education can provide for them. Thank you so much to educators from preschool through universities. Family and teachers make a difference forever and you can too.

Contents

Foreword by Sara Rimm-Kaufman

It's 2025 and the United States is truly a nation of immigrants. Let's start with the numbers. Roughly 15% of people living in the U.S. are immigrants and about 20% of migrants in the world find their way to the U.S. (Pew Research Center, 2024). Among the immigrants in the U.S., roughly 23% were from Mexico with 6%, 5%, and 4% from India, China, and the Philippines, respectively, based on 2022 figures. In public schools, roughly 11% of students are English Learners (EL) with tremendous range across states. For example, fewer than 1% of students are (EL) in West Virginia and over 20% of students are (EL) in Texas. I share these numbers for two reasons—these figures remind us of how common it is to be newly arrived in the U.S., but also because of the way these numbers tie into my mother's story about her own immigrant experience.

My mother's family arrived here in the U.S. in 1929. During the 1920s in the U.S., between 10% and 15% of people were immigrants, but that figure was declining as borders closed and people were turned away. My mother's parents and older sister made it to the U.S., as did two of the families of my mother's uncles. My grandmother and nine siblings remained in Uruguay and Argentina because the United States closed the doors on immigrants. Sadly, some cousins stayed in Latvia and may have perished in World War II.

What stands out in my mind is that people who are immigrants are taking a huge leap of faith.

Sometimes they are pushed out of their countries because of violence, few employment opportunities, corruption, racism, or poverty, and other times they are pulled to the U.S. for the hope of a better life regardless of their circumstances in their home countries. In my family's case, we believe they felt both "pushed" and "pulled," but we'll never know for sure. Regardless,

immigrants like my grandparents leave all they know with the faith that the social systems in the

U.S. will keep them afloat until they can get their feet under them here in this new country. In January 2025, I fear that many of these social systems are increasingly tenuous, and the U.S. will become a less hospitable place for immigrants.

The immigrant experience can be viewed from economic, sociological, or political points of view. I am writing this foreword from the perspective of a developmental psychologist, and many ideas in my field that relate to immigration and connect to my family's heritage. Here, I've chosen just two ideas that seem important in understanding how youth adjust to being new Americans and how those of us who have been here for generations can support newcomers.

Homophily and Propinquity

The first idea relates to a universal attribute that all people have. Everyone has a natural tendency to become friends with people who are similar to them and who spend time near them.

Psychologists even have names for these ideas: homophily, which means a preference for people who are like you and propinquity, which refers to partiality for people near you (Echols & Graham, 2013; McPherson, 2001). Reflect for a minute about your closest friends. They might be the same race or religion as you—that's homophily. Perhaps they live next door, ten minutes away, or work in an office down the hall—that's propinquity. These tendencies are typical, normal, and part of the human condition—for good or for bad—as we will discuss next.

In the context of immigrant and EL students, homophily is likely to take hold. Immigrant students are likely to seek out peers who share their linguistic, cultural, or experiential backgrounds. These connections can provide a sense of comfort and mutual understanding. Likewise, propinquity occurs naturally based on where students live and go to school. Immigrant groups often gravitate toward one or two neighborhoods within a town or city, making it more likely that friendships will form among those who live just a few blocks apart. These natural tendencies lend themselves to healthy peer relationships and it's very important for identity development for youth to share experiences with people who are similar to them and live near them.

However, these special relationships are not enough for youth to thrive. Youth also need to learn how to get along with people who are different from them and are not necessarily friendships of convenience. To make this happen, educators and parents need to work very hard to help youth stretch and get to know people who differ from them. It is important that youth experience cross-cultural interactions to promote broader social integration and cultural exchange. These experiences cultivate curiosity in others and can help people realize the common humanity in people which can be very healthy for society.

There are some recommendations that I have for families and teachers related to this idea. Schools are often ethnically diverse and I recommend educators group students intentionally to allow youth to work with people who are different from them. Schools can use books, recent news stories from the community, and incorporate projects into instruction that represent various cultures and can help create familiarity with the cultures of the new immigrants in the school. Often, families of immigrant youth feel uncomfortable in their child's school setting, where the culture or language may be unfamiliar to them. Educators can reach out specifically to these families and make them feel welcome.

The take-home message here is that it is essential to stretch children away from their natural tendencies of homophily and propinquity so they get to know people who are different from them and may not live next door. Ultimately, these experiences of interacting with people who are different from them lead to the development of perspective-taking, social awareness, and effective communication.

Yosso's Cultural Wealth Theory

Yosso's Cultural Wealth Theory (2005) takes a strength-based perspective on understanding the various forms of capital that these communities possess. By definition, capital refers to a type of wealth that is not in the form of money or other assets. The Cultural Wealth Theory identifies six types of capital and I define and describe these below and give examples that apply to immigrant families.

○ **Aspirational Capital:** The resilience and hope that students maintain despite challenges. Many families have spent months or years in refugee camps before coming to the U.S. Their ability to be resilient during very tough times and maintain hope for themselves and their children serves as aspirational capital that can serve them well during challenging times.

○ **Linguistic Capital:** The skills and social advantages gained from being bilingual or multilingual. In so many countries in the world, children learn two or three languages with no problem. In fact, the U.S. is a little odd in that we have so many monolingual people. New immigrants often have an advantage in this area because they know more than one language. That can be seen as an asset, not a deficit, that can help people thrive.

○ **Familial Capital:** The cultural knowledge and sense of community nurtured through family connections. Often, immigrants arrive in family groups and are brought to the U.S. by family already here. The tight connections that can occur in family groups can be a tremendous resource for youths' psychological health.

○ **Social Capital:** The networks of people and community resources that provide support. How do new immigrants find jobs? How do they get around in places without public transportation if they cannot drive? In essence, immigrants need to rely on people in the community and they quickly learn to leverage their social connections to create a good life in the U.S.

○ **Navigational Capital:** The ability to maneuver through social institutions, including educational systems. Consider the many different systems that immigrants need to manage in coming to the U.S. First, immigration services, then travel, then adjustment to a new city with new customs and cultures. Often, families gain remarkable skills in navigating challenging situations as they make all these adjustments and adaptations.

○ **Resistant Capital:** The knowledge and skills developed through oppositional behavior that challenges inequality. Immigrants in the U.S. are living in places that were designed for white people who have been in the U.S. for long periods of time. That means immigrants need to break a lot of "glass ceilings" to make it in the U.S. Kudos to the immigrants who have the courage to push back against oppressive systems. For those of us working with immigrants, it seems more essential than ever to support these efforts.

I call attention to these forms of capital because they reframe our thinking about what it means to be an immigrant. New immigrants are coming in with so many strengths, often based on hard- earned lessons in their home countries. These strengths can be noticed and leveraged as they create productive lives for themselves in the U.S. Schools can identify and build from these sources of capital to help students and their families adjust and grow.

These ideas bring me back to my own family. My mom spent countless hours at the YMHA in high school with mostly Jewish kids who were like her and lived near her, showing both homophily and propinquity. My grandparents owned a grocery store in Perth Amboy. Although they had little formal education, they had vast aspirational, linguistic, familial, social, and navigational capital. So much has changed from the 1920s-1930s to now, yet the inclusion of immigrants into U.S. society continues to be an incredible source of wealth for us all.

My mom's story of her life is remarkable to me. Her story conveys important messages about hope, risk-taking, education, and family. At this moment in history, as we see anti-immigrant sentiment growing, I hope this book will inspire readers to be curious, foster inclusivity, and offer support for people coming to the U.S. so they, too, can live the American Dream.

References:

Echols, L., & Graham, S. (2013). Birds of a different feather: How do cross-ethnic friends flock together?. Merrill-Palmer Quarterly, 59(4), 461-488.

McPherson, M., Smith-Lovin, L., & Cook, J. M. (2001). Birds of a feather: Homophily in social networks. Annual review of sociology, 27(1), 415-444.

Pew Research Center (2024). What the data says about immigrants in the U.S. Retrieved from: https://www.pewresearch.org/short-reads/2024/09/27/key-findings-about-us-immigrants/

Yosso, T. J. (2005). Whose culture has capital? A critical race theory discussion of community cultural wealth. Race ethnicity and education, 8(1), 69-91.

Introduction to Students and Teachers

At age 89, as I sit in our Naples, Florida condo, pen in hand, I wonder how I managed to live such an extraordinarily fulfilling life. I wonder how it could all have happened and how I can say so many thank-yous to all the wonderful people who encouraged me. Even in my wildest childhood dreams, I never could have imagined having such an amazing family, building such an extraordinary career, living so many beautiful adventures, and positively influencing the lives of thousands of children and adults. I hope that by sharing my life experiences I can inspire new Americans to dream of life successes and work toward accomplishment, fulfillment, and contribution.

Only in America could it happen that a fearful, shy immigrant child—raised in a poor neighborhood by parents with serious health problems during the frightening days of World War II—emerge from such low self-expectations to live a life as beautiful, challenging, intrinsically interesting, and wondrous as mine. I've traveled the world and spoken to literally millions on TV, national radio, online and in giant auditoriums and cruise ships. I have truly lived an American Dream.

Our children convinced me to at least write some of it down, and as I wrote, I remembered so much more again—the fears, the challenges, the exciting victories, as well as the defeats and disappointments. Mostly I remembered so many of the people who made my extraordinarily fulfilling life possible.

Unfortunately, I'm sure that I have also forgotten some, and I apologize if I missed any of those wonderful people. How can I say thank you to so many? My parents, sisters, in-laws, many teachers, my school counselor Mrs. Herbert, college and graduate school professors, mentors, agents, television and radio colleagues and producers, employees, neighbors and friends, students, and—last but not least—my children, grandchildren, and now even my great-grandchildren.

For those of you who choose to read my story, I hope you find inspiration and motivation—just as I did from those whose magical words guided me forward. What you learn in school can inspire you to find a fulfilling career where you, too, can help others to make a positive difference to our world.

CHAPTER 1

My Family Heritage

About My Parents

My mother was Reva (Rivka) Cisser. She married my father, Harry (Hirsh) Barkan, and became Reva Barkan. The story of how my parents met became a family legend and a bit of a miracle. Both my father's brothers, David and Phillip, were killed quickly after being drafted into the Czar's army. (That part is so sad.) My father's sister, Ida, had secretly arranged to escape to the United States. My dad was, therefore, forced to stay in Dvinsk, Latvia to care for his mother, Reva (the same name as our mom). She had terminal tuberculosis. His dad, Velvel, had already passed away. Thus, when he came of age, he was also drafted into the Czar's Army. The Czar was very antisemitic. Many young Jewish boys were drafted and considered "cannon fodder" for his army. My dad's hand was almost immediately wounded in battle, and he feared that he, too, would soon be killed if he didn't desert the army. He told us the story of his escape many times.

> *"I escaped overnight and crawled on my belly across a huge farm field to a safe house the first night. Then the second night I again crawled on my belly all the way to Riga, Latvia."*

Riga was not yet under Russian domination, so he was safe from the army. Imagine how lonely he must have felt with no family in Latvia. That's when he met my mother. I can still hear him now telling the story to us as children.

Mommy had just broken up with a boyfriend she had gone out with for four years, and I fell in love with her. I chased her and chased her and chased her and would not let her go until she agreed to marry me. I was so in love with her.

My father came from Dvinsk, Latvia, which was a big city. He didn't talk much about his city, and I was never there. The city has been renamed Daugavpils. My mother, who lived in Riga, described it as a beautiful city and told us how they loved ice skating on the Baltic Sea when it was frozen. She said she ice skated holding on to a chair. My mother had very few years of formal education. My father had quite a few and was educated in Judaism and knew Hebrew and Yiddish very well. In those times boys received a full Jewish education, but girls were not expected to have any education. I don't think my mother could read or "spell" (her word) in any language very well.

I remember when my father used to read letters to my mother from the Yiddish newspaper. He read for their entertainment. My father would read Questions/Answer advice columns, and they would talk about the answers and laugh and talk about people's lives. I think that in some ways, they were trying to figure out what people were like in America to better understand the culture.

After my father went to night school and things were going well, my mother went to night school, and she learned to read a little bit of English too. My parents would always talk with pride about other members of our family who had come to the U.S. and whose children were now teachers or librarians. One cousin was a doctor, another a dentist, and even as a child, I could sense that our family deeply revered educated people. I naturally assumed they expected us to pursue an education as well. Even though neither of my parents read English books, we had a few in our house, and we all read. It was very clear that my parents valued education.

My Grandparents

I never met any of my grandparents. Three had passed away before I was born. One grandfather, Yitzhak, lived in Uruguay. My mother waited eagerly for his letters. She cried as she read them. She missed her family so much. She wrote to him in Yiddish. My father's father was Velvel, and his wife was Reva. My mother's father was Yitzak, and my mother's mother was Simcha. Simcha means

"joyous celebration or party." I was named after her. I'm sure I inherited a love for family togetherness from my mother and grandmother. Each time we get our family together for a celebration, I recall with perfect clarity my mother doing the same. It feels so natural that it must be genetic.

Aunts, Uncles, and Cousins by the Dozens

My mother came from a family of nine children. Her father and most of the siblings could not get sponsorship to come to the United States, but they had to leave Riga due to fears of antisemitism. When my Uncle Max later visited us from Argentina, he told me how one of his brothers tried to falsify a passport to escape Latvia, was caught, and sent to jail. The siblings somehow got him out of jail on bail or illegally, but then they had to leave Latvia, or they would also have been jailed. The only country that would accept them was Uruguay.

They went by ship to Montevideo and some of them later moved to Buenos Aires, Argentina.

My mother would cry because she missed her family. She missed her siblings and father. She felt so isolated from so much of her family. That may be part of why she emphasized love of family so much. Many years later, she did see Uncle Max and Uncle Moishe. They visited us with their wives in New Jersey. They and their children came afterwards several times while both our parents were still alive.

I have made two visits to South America to visit our family. The first one was with my sister, Vivian, and the second one, about 10 years later, was with my sister, Frances. On that last trip, we actually visited with 36 cousins in Montevideo and Buenos Aires. Some cousins had moved to Colombia, South America. Our family settled in South America because the United States closed doors on immigrants from Latvia.

My mother's brothers (our uncles) included Moishe, Berl, and Max, who lived in South America, and Hymie and Robert, who came to the United States.

One of mother's sisters, Lena, died very young—at age 50—from breast cancer in South America. Another older sister, whose name I don't recall, also died of cancer. Her sisters died very young. Her brothers lived very long, into their late 80s, except for one, Robert, who died of a burst appendix in the Bronx, New York at age 50. We had lots of cousins in the Bronx on my mother's side, but most very close cousins didn't make it to this country. My mother's most frequent message that I carry to my own children was the importance of staying close to family.

Even though my father's only living sibling, Ida, had caused him to be very angry because she left him stranded and, therefore, caused him to be drafted, my mother insisted that he get over his anger at his sister and be nice to her and her family. We became very close to Aunt Idy and Uncle Challie Toborowsky. Their son, Bobby, and I were almost as close as siblings.

We were really close to my mom's family. We would visit the Bronx by taking a ferry to Staten Island, then a train across Staten Island to St. George, followed by another ferry to Manhattan, and finally the subway into the Bronx. They would come to visit us, too. I was the youngest of the children, so none of the cousins were my age.

My sisters were nearer to their ages (Hermina, Bob, and Connie), and they had much fun together.

Our families had to leave Riga because there was antisemitism by the Czar in the entire area. If they had managed to outlive the Czar's antisemitism, the Nazis would have eradicated most of them during

World War II. I visited Riga many years later, and I saw the wooded area where the Nazis lead 10,000 Jews and shot them all at gunpoint. It's likely that is what would have happened to us if my parents had stayed in Riga, and I'm thankful that they immigrated in 1930. As young adults, they had one baby, Rose, who died at the age of one of diphtheria in Latvia. My sister, Vivian, was 11 months old when they immigrated to the United States. They were sponsored by Rose Pargot, my father's first cousin. We are forever appreciative of her help. Incidentally, Cousin Rose Pargot lived a long life.

She died at 103. Aunt Frances and I joke about planning to live as long as she did.

We're trying. J

For Jews to immigrate to the United States, they needed a sponsor—someone who would guarantee they had employment and would not become dependent on government assistance. When my parents came here, my father took a job in a pocketbook (handbag) factory on an assembly line, and that assured them that he could make a living. He only worked five days a week. Also, I remember that he would take us to the "movies" every Saturday and we would see cowboy pictures. I don't think I really understood them, but I loved going with my daddy and sisters.

Chapter 2

Our Homes While Growing Up

Our First Home

We settled in Perth Amboy, New Jersey. The first home I remember was on the second floor of a house at 405 Park Avenue in Perth Amboy, NJ. Although I was very young, I remember some of the house clearly. We had two male borders living in our house with us. My mother also cooked meals for them. That income was used to help pay our rent. One of them was named Jack. After he was no longer a border, he and his wife became good friends to our family. I don't remember the other border's name.

I remember several things from that first home we lived in. I was very young, three or four years old. There was an attic entrance in the ceiling of a closet, and my sisters told me all sorts of mysterious stories about what they imagined was happening up there. We never really knew because we couldn't get up there, but I was very frightened of it. The second event I remember was a strange accident. My sister, Frances, and I share the same birthday, so my mother was making us each a birthday cake in the kitchen. I was looking over the railing on our second-floor porch and leaned over too far and fell. There was a fence on the ground below and, fortunately, my skirt got caught on that fence, so I was saved by it and never hit the ground. I had only a small scratch on my leg which my mother covered with mercurochrome. I can still remember hanging from the fence. I was terrified and so was everyone else.

I have a third positive and cute childhood memory while living in that house. Our older siblings decided to arrange a pretend wedding for me and Benjy. This was even before kindergarten, and my older sisters and his siblings decided we should get married. I always laugh about that, because developmentally, girls and boys play together in kindergarten—and then, typically and temporarily, in first grade, girls say, "boys, yuck" and boys say, "girls, yuck." Benjy and I really never stayed friends even after our "cute pretend marriage," but I do remember the backyard wedding.

Our Second Home Behind Our Grocery Store— 195 Broad Street

Although our parents came here in the heart of the depression and we were very poor, I didn't know I was poor. After my dad worked in the factory for several years, my parents borrowed money from a cousin, Jake Katz, and bought a little "mom-and-pop" grocery store. They didn't actually buy the building, just the ownership of the store. We moved to the apartment behind the store. It had two bedrooms, one very tiny bathroom, a living room and a kitchen. My two sisters and I all slept in the same bedroom on two twin beds. I shared a bed with Frances. My father's elderly aunt slept in the other bedroom because our parents were caring for her. Our parents slept on a pullout sofa in the living room, and we all shared that one little bathroom. We had to turn on a little hot water heater in the bathroom that heated the water before we'd take a shower or a bath so the water would be hot enough. We had a coal stove to heat our house. I remember my dad going down to the basement and taking ashes out of the stove.

The store was right up front with only a curtain that separated our home from the store. My mother and father both worked in the store. Their store hours were 6:00 a.m. till 10:00 p.m., six days a week. On Sunday, they began at 6:00 a.m. but they closed the store at 6:00 p.m. and had "poker" card parties with their friends.

We all used to help in the store. My special time was Sunday morning because that was a busy time. I would get up early and help my dad sort the Sunday newspapers and wait on customers. When I was done for the day and told my dad I was leaving, he would jokingly add "Lincoln freed the slaves."

Our "mom-and-pop" grocery store sold delicatessen meats, fresh fruits and vegetables, canned goods, ice cream, candy, and cigarettes. My mother and my father worked together. My father got up early in the morning and stayed till night, but he took a nap in the afternoon when my mother would take over so they could keep the store going. They made a living, and we never lacked for food. Drake's Yankee Doodles and Devil Dogs were my favorite cakes, and I often had them for breakfast. We scooped lots of ice cream, too, and had too many penny candies. It's no wonder I had early teeth cavities.

My father was very good at languages, and we lived in an immigrant neighborhood. There were very few Jews but many Christian immigrants from Poland, Italy, Russia and Greece. My father seemed to know everyone's language. I don't think he had full language capacity, but he said "hello" when people came in and "How are you?" typically in the languages of the customers.

Our store didn't have a cash register at first. My dad would write the prices on a bag and then add them up in his head. He was very quick and honest, and when someone didn't have quite enough money and they said they'd pay him later, he would typically say, "I'll mark it down in my book." To us kids, he would say, "I'll mark it on the ice." I did, as a child, ask him what he meant by that. He explained that the debt would melt away like the ice. He was a very generous, kind and funny guy, but he wasn't a risk taker. My mother was and encouraged him to get new products in the store and came up with ideas for small expansions and adventures.

Yes, one other thing I forgot. We did have some cats in our store, but they were not our pet friends. Their job was to keep the mouse population from multiplying. I wasn't supposed to touch or play with them.

Our Own Home—205 Broad Street

My parents worked hard together, and they wanted to earn their dream, a home of their own. They finally bought a home that was actually a three-family house. We moved into the first-floor apartment, and the second and third floors had renters. They used the rent to pay the monthly mortgage payments. Our family was very excited. By that time, I was about 11 years old and in 6th grade. My sisters were excited because finally we could each have our own bedroom. I pretended I was excited, too, but didn't tell anyone how frightened I really was. I remember how terrified I was as if it was just yesterday. I was to sleep alone in my own bedroom for the first time in my life. I would lie awake at night and look at the walls and think they were moving. I also thought there were ghosts in the closet, and it took me quite a few weeks to adjust to sleeping alone. Our new home was really nice with lots of large mirrors and carpets and beautiful new furniture. My parents spent a lot of time fixing it up. I would play music on the phonograph and watch myself dancing in the large mirror. I just loved to dance.

Early Vacations

We did have brief family vacations, but they were usually without my dad. I remember that we went to a farm in the countryside. That was because my oldest sister, Vivian, was too underweight and the doctor recommended a dairy farm so she would be better nourished (with lots of milk, cheese and ice cream). I remember the farm vaguely and recall lying on a blanket on the grass before I could walk. Later we vacationed at the Jersey Shore (in Bradley Beach) for about a week during each summer. We'd rent a house there and share the kitchen with someone else. We had distant cousins, the Tessels, whose children (Helen and Mildred) came too. Again, I was the youngest of the cousins, so my sisters had cousins to play with, but I didn't. I loved the beach and the boardwalk and Asbury Park for the amusement park rides. Those are very, very nice memories, although the vacations were brief.

Chapter 3

My Before School Years and Friends

When I was still a "little kid", I had some very close friends in our neighborhood. We were a Jewish family, but my best friend, Teresa, was Catholic and went to St. Mary's Catholic School. Her parents were divorced, and she lived with her mother and grandmother. Most people assume that divorce was not common in that generation, but it was frequent in our neighborhood.

My other closest friend was Marilyn. Her mother was Jewish, but her father was Catholic, and they too were divorced. She lived with her mother. In our neighborhood, we had very few intact families. Most of the children I went to school with and some of my closest friends, Manny and Jerry, came from single-parent homes.

Later when I was about 11 years old, I went with my closest friend, Teresa, who was Catholic, to a little store in the neighborhood once. We were hanging around with some neighbor girls and boys. I came home and told my mother what we did. All we were doing was singing, drinking sodas and talking. The next day my mother announced, "That's over. You can't hang around with Teresa and non- Jewish boys." She explained that now that boys were involved, I was to socialize with only Jewish friends, and I could find them at the "Y". The YMHA (Young Men's Hebrew Association) was our recreation center for Jewish children, teens and even young adults. We roller skated in the gym, and I had a whole Jewish community at the Y. In the summers I attended the Y Day Camp.

I remember when I was about eight years old, I won a Leadership Award. The problem was that I didn't understand what the word "leadership" meant, but I felt a little special and scared. At day camp, we went to the Y indoor swimming pool. The person in charge of the pool was named "Heckie Plane." He taught us how to swim. We also had activities at Roosevelt Park. Until I was eleven or so, I socialized in both communities but then my mother forbade it. "Now the Y is your community." She said I could still be friendly with Theresa, but she was supposed to be with Catholics. My mother never said anything bad about her, only that I must be part of the Jewish community. I think my parents were very afraid of antisemitism. Here's what happened to me.

I was walking in our neighborhood with Theresa and Marilyn, and we saw a boy coming towards us. Theresa whispered in my ear that he didn't like Jews. I wasn't worried because he looked small enough so I could protect myself. We kept walking toward each other. Then he pointed to me and said, "You're a Jew; you're a Christ killer, put up your dukes!" I put up my little fists and he promptly punched me out. Wow—I can feel the pain now. I screamed and cried and ran all the way home to my parents. My friends told them what happened. Then my parents talked to his parents, and they said they punished him and that it wouldn't happen again. I stayed far away from him, but I was terrified of antisemitism after that.

The "Y" provided wonderful and enriching fun for us. We went roller skating in the gym and had dances on the roof, nature hikes and art classes. Our "Y" was still on the "wrong side" (the poor side) of town. The "right" side of town was where the upper middle-class families lived. The Jewish families there had grandparents who were immigrants, but their parents were brought up in the U.S. Most had fathers who had gone to college. We had a wonderful Jewish community, and it was very important to me. I met nice quality kids there but not until grammar school.

Birth Order Matters

I was a good kid as "baby" of the family. I would watch my older sisters get into trouble and I remember thinking "I'm not gonna do that." Both of my sisters smoked, and they even smoked in their bedrooms behind closed doors. My parents were furious with them because my parents did not smoke. I wouldn't have touched a cigarette. My sisters went out on dates with soldiers and sailors (during World War II) and came home late at night. My oldest sister, Vivian, especially got in trouble with my parents. Vivian was very smart and had skipped a grade when she was younger. By high school she did very poorly because she didn't study, didn't work hard and did too much socializing. Her friends and she probably had some alcoholic drinks that they weren't supposed to have. I don't really know exactly, but I know that I would hear them come home late and my mother and father would worry and scold them. Each time my sisters were scolded, I renewed my vows not to ever smoke or drink. I was clearly determined to be a "goody-goody."

My second sister didn't get into quite as much trouble, but she smoked, too. I felt very close to both my sisters. They were mostly wonderful and kind to me because I was the baby. Sometimes they would get really angry when I didn't have to do the dishes and they would say something like, "How come Simi doesn't have to do anything?" And my mother would say, "She's studying" and I would call out, "I'm doing my homework." As a child psychologist, I'm very aware of how sibling rivalry and sibling personas affect every child. My persona was definitely of, "I've got to be the good kid and I'd better study hard." I had a peer group of kids who were good students, and I was one too. Neither of my sisters went to college, and I never expected to go to college either because my parents could not even consider paying tuition. My mother's message was clear. "You should marry an educated man, but girls don't have to go to college." Another clear message I received was that once we married, we should love our husband's parents as our own—because they raised a wonderful husband for us. That was a very positive message I accepted.

I think we were a loving family. My sisters cared about me. They advised me on the right style of clothes to wear and helped me figure out social things. They were very nice to me. We ate together behind the store, or we ate in the house. My father and mother would take turns eating with us because someone had to be in the store. We didn't have a lot of fancy food, but we'd have family dinners on Sundays if a family member from New York came to see us. My mother was a good Jewish cook, and we had plenty of food to eat. As fresh vegetables became more available, she would even cook broccoli and Brussels sprouts. We had lots of fresh fruit and vegetables.

During my teen years, my father's Parkinson's Disease developed and got worse, and my mother had colorectal cancer, so they had to give up the store. My dad went into a nursing home because there was nobody to take care of him when my mother became ill and later died of cancer. Before my mom got sick, she took an extra job in a Smith Street store because our store wasn't bringing in enough money. She was a saleswoman. Although my parents belonged to an Orthodox synagogue, my mother said, "I'm not that Orthodox because we work on Shabbos (Saturdays)."

Our family store was open on Saturdays, too. They only closed the store on Rosh Hashana and Yom Kippur. They were even open during Passover. We'd have our Seders late after the store closed. My father was not very religious at all, although he had lots of Jewish learning and even worked as a volunteer cantor for a few years. They were absolutely united in their wish that we were to marry Jewish boys. That was very clear. My parents kept a kosher home. My mother would cook on Friday, for Shabbos. On Friday when we came home the house was always clean. I could smell both the cleanliness and the delicious chicken baking in the oven. It was our Friday Shabbos dinner and our leftover lunch on Saturday because my mother wouldn't turn on the gas during Shabbos. She had to work because she said, "God would understand you have to work, so you do it." Our parents belonged to an Orthodox synagogue with many immigrant families. It was much less Orthodox than those of today.

CHAPTER 4

My School Years

#1 School—Kindergarten through Grade Five

Kindergarten started for our generation at age four. I remember my first day because I cried when my mother left me at school. No one seemed very worried, so I eventually stopped. My teacher was Miss Moore. She had white hair and a very quiet voice. We could order drinks--either white or chocolate milk. We only went for half a day and in the afternoon.

One day we sat in a circle and Miss Moore asked us what we had eaten for lunch. I had eaten chicken noodle soup, but in Yiddish my mother called it "lukchen soup." I was afraid to answer because I wasn't sure whether "lukchen soup" was the English or Yiddish name for it. Tears filled my eyes as I named my soup. I don't remember a correction—all that angst for nothing.

Toward the end of the school year a different teacher met with me and gave me a test. Afterwards, Miss Moore told my mother I could skip sub-primary and go right to first grade. I started first grade and was trying my best, but the principal, Miss Dorsey, called my mother to say that Arthur Aneckstein's mother didn't think it was fair for me to skip a grade when Arthur couldn't. So, the principal said she had to put me back to sub-primary. They seated me next to Lynell. She was bigger than me and she pinched me really hard. I didn't cry but I was scared. The teacher, Miss Feldman, changed my seat and then I was okay. I was always afraid of Lynell after that.

My next teachers were Miss Warga (Grade 1), Miss Zanzelarri (Grade 2), Miss Garretson (Grade 3). I loved school and got all A's and 100's.

Miss Shoobridge (Grade 4) was my favorite teacher. I just loved her. She told us about her travels and the national parks and the beauty of nature. After lunch, the globe and maps came out and she introduced us to the big world. We saw pictures of birds from the Audubon Society, and she gave Joan and me some special work in a "hard" workbook. I told her I thought it was too hard for us, but she said it was alright to make a mistake as long as we tried our best. So, Joan and I worked together on our hard work, and we felt really smart, happy and challenged. Miss Shoobridge encouraged my writing, and I started writing my first stories in her class. She was the kind of teacher that anyone who had special needs or special challenges was provided for. We threw her a surprise party because we truly thought she was the best teacher we ever had—and we believed she felt the same about our class. I don't think we really were but that's what we thought. You might notice by the "Miss" that teachers were rarely married in those days.

My very closest friend in elementary school was Joan. Her father was a doctor, and her mother was a stay-at-home mom. They did not live in our neighborhood, but I met her at school. Her mom had a college education, and they were upper middle class. I'm still in touch with Joan today, although we were best friends in third through fifth grade. She became a Reading teacher and continues to teach students, although she is way past retirement. She visited us in Key Largo a few times.

Another close friend was Barbara. I didn't get along as well with her in 4th grade because I was afraid that she would steal Joan away from me. We became good friends again in high school.

In 5th grade, my teacher was Miss Canse, and I think Manny Marks was my boyfriend. That meant we chased each other on the playground. Also, on the way home from school, we chased each other at the very windy "five corners" in Perth Amboy." Cousin Bobby went to my school, too, and sometimes we walked home together and ran through the windy corners. What fun we had running in the wind!

Our school did not serve lunches, so we all went home for lunch and came back for recess time on the playground before the second half of our day. One day Bobby came running home with me to eat in our home behind the store.

Bobby's mother worked in a factory during the war, so she was not at home for lunch. Snow flurries swirled all around us, so Bobby and I began singing: "Oh the weather outside is frightful, but the fire is so delightful,,, turn the lights way down low, let it snow, let it snow, let it snow."

As we entered our house with those last lines, my mom looked at us both and said, "Why no lettuce?" We burst out laughing and explained the words of the song to my mom. She just didn't know about popular music.

Extra-Curricular Activities

In addition to going to school daily, I went to after-school classes at Sholem Aleichem Folk School #7. We had about five or six students per class. There I learned to read, write and understand Yiddish. I learned lots of Purim and Chanukah and Shabbos songs in Yiddish too, and we put on performances and plays in Yiddish for our parents. I was always really nervous before performances. No one worried about that and everyone applauded afterwards. It felt good, and acting in plays helped me feel confident and smart.

I also took weekly piano lessons from Miss Ford, and we put on recitals every year for our parents. I even played in competitions doing both solos and duets with a boy piano player whose name was Gregg. I don't think I was very good, but I did get to learn about Chopin and Mozart and Beethoven and Bach and so I've always appreciated classical music.

Speaking of Gregg and piano duets, let me share the cause of my fear of dogs with you. I would ride to Gregg's house on my bike. One day, on the way home a dog chased me and bit my ankle. Yikes, an ambulance came and took me to the hospital. I think they gave me a rabies shot, too. Of course, I recovered quickly, but I certainly continued my fear of barking dogs.

I also remember that I wanted to take tap dancing lessons, but I'm guessing my mother thought I had too much to do. I danced in front of the mirror in our house anyway. I loved to dance.

World War II Surrounded Us

During the time I was in elementary school, World War II was taking place.

I was playing at my friend Theresa's house when the attack on Pearl Harbor was announced on the radio. We had no TV then. I remember it clearly. Theresa asked her mother why everyone was so upset. Her mother told her that war was declared, and our fathers would go to fight the war and many fathers would die. Theresa's father went into the Navy, but fortunately, he did not die. I remember when he visited her in his Navy uniform. I remember most that suddenly; our world was different and very scary.

My father was too old to be drafted but he became an air raid warden. When there was an air raid drill, he would go out with a special helmet with a light on and a giant flashlight. He would walk the streets to be sure no one was out and all the lights in homes were off. Everyone else had to go into whatever house they were near. We turned off all lights and closed windows and pulled down shades so no airplane would see our homes. Then we listened to the radio until we heard an "all clear" signal.

I was very frightened during the air raids. I would imagine bombers overhead dropping bombs or submarines in Raritan Bay with bombs. The air raid drills in schools were even scarier. We went to the halls in the basement of the school and were never sure of what was really going to happen until we would hear the all clear signal.

In school we learned about the war and how to help the war effort. We had ration books for things like sugar and coffee and milk, so birthday cakes were really a luxury. We collected old newspapers in the neighborhood in a little red wagon for the war effort. I'm not sure how they were used.

We sang victory songs like "Let's remember Pearl Harbor" as my children all remember me singing to them on Pearl Harbor Day.

> Let's remember Pearl Harbor, as we go to meet the foe.

> Let's remember Pearl Harbor, as we did the Alamo. We will always remember how they died for liberty. Let's remember Pearl Harbor and go on to victory.

We saw silver stars on people's windows for soldiers who were fighting and gold stars for soldiers who had died. A man wandered the streets near us, and I

was afraid of him. My mother said not to be afraid because he was "shell shocked" and wouldn't hurt anyone. I was afraid because he looked strange and mean. They were scary times, and I thought that ghosts and Nazis lived in our closets during the nights.

Parkinson's Disease

My dad was only in his 40s when he contracted Parkinson's Disease. At that time, doctors didn't know what it was. For two to three years, he went from doctor to doctor because no one could name his tremor or predict how long it would last or what caused it. Finally, they hypothesized that it resulted from the flu epidemic of 1918 because there were others who also had the same symptoms. I'm not sure if they know yet what causes Parkinson's Disease. My dad continued working in the store but couldn't write the prices on the bags because of his tremor. He used to memorize prices and add them up in his head until they finally got a cash register and they updated the store to a more modern checkout style.

The Grammar School Years

In 6th grade I went to Grammar School. We had also moved to our new home by then. It was only one and a half blocks from home to school, and I wasn't afraid to walk to school anymore. Our school, however, had its own mysteries and stories. It was located on Barracks Street because the building had been a barracks for World War I soldiers. No one was allowed to enter the basement, and there were stories that soldiers had died there during bombings—and that their bodies were still down there. I didn't spend much time worrying about that except maybe around Halloween when ghosts were in style.

Mostly I was very happy at grammar school. I got all A's and had plenty of friends—mostly girlfriends, though there were a few boys I'd chase around the playground—like Manny and Sandy.

I liked math and writing and doing projects, but I also remember how hard it was for me to get started—to get the "perfect idea." I guess I was perfectionistic. In 8th grade I had to write a report on the slave trade from Africa. I wrote it as a story as if I were a slave coming over on a ship from Africa—about the crowded conditions and my fears as a child coming to America. Miss Geery asked me to read my report to the class. I watched my hands trembling as I read. When I finished, there was a strange silence. Then Miss Geery said, "Now class, what do you think of that?" The whole class applauded, and I was in shock. I got an A+. I think that started my writing life, although I had many ups and downs about writing after that, and I had so little confidence. It never occurred to me that I would ever be an author.

As to math, I got the highest math score in my grade when I took the pre- algebra test in 8th grade. It was a very large middle school, so that was pretty exciting for me. I'm not sure what happened to that great math ability, but I lost it along the way.

Another unusual incident happened in 8th grade. A lazy under-achieving boy named Larry got into trouble for something. I don't remember what he did, but the teacher suspended him from school and threatened to expel him. His friends thought the teachers weren't fair to Larry and decided that they should march in protest to the principal's office in support of Larry. Surprise, surprise. I joined and helped lead the march, but I was frightened. We came to the principal's office and together we said, "You're not being fair to Larry. He didn't mean to get into trouble."

The principal was angry and said, "Stop immediately. You will all stay after school," and then he further said, "And you, Sylvia, you are a good student. What are you doing with this crowd?" I meekly answered, "I didn't think it was fair." He said, "Sylvia, go back to your class," and I, Sylvia, with tears in my eyes, humbly went back to my class and didn't get the punishment the other students did, although the principal's words felt like punishment enough.

Dancing at School

I remember learning to dance and doing cheerleading while I was at Grammar School. At school, in gym class wearing gym suits we learned lots of steps. At the Y, I think we had a co-ed dance class where we learned to Polka, Waltz, Two Step and, most fun of all, to Jitterbug. Our actual dances didn't take place until high school, but we had lessons.

My sister, Vivian, did sewing and she made me some really nice clothes. When I'd get invited to a party, I had pretty ballerina skirts that she made and that everyone admired. I was accepted by the kids who were really good students, and they really liked me, and I liked them.

At the Y we learned to do cheerleading for our boys' basketball team. We made up our own cheers and they weren't very fancy, but we had fun. Girls also learned to play basketball, but because we were girls we didn't have sports teams at the Y or in school. Cheering was the best we could do.

Now I know you've all seen me tap dance to East Side, West Side. Bernice Eaton, my black friend, taught a group of us that dance and we danced it at a school show. I still remember all the steps. You all know how I love dancing, and now you know that my love of dancing really started when I was in grammar school.

Girl Scouts

Girl Scouts had been important to my sisters and so I assumed that I, too, would soon be a Girl Scout. I joined as soon as I could. There were no Brownie Scouts in our day, so Girl Scouts belonged to the middle grades. I remember we did crafts, and I worked on badges, and I think I worked my way up to a First Class Scout. For certain, I mastered the sale of plenty of Girl Scout cookies.

Girl Scout Camp in Massachusetts with my friend, Joan, was my first trip away from home without my parents. We went there on a train to Boston, and Joan's relatives picked us up at the station and delivered us to camp in the "rumble seat" of their car. I can still remember the excitement of my first and only ride in a rumble seat—exciting, scary, likely not even very safe, but we loved it. I suppose it was safer than riding in the back of Uncle Charlie's open pickup truck sitting on orange crates. The biggest difference in Massachusetts was that it was the very first time I had gone away without my mother. It was a true adventure. I loved the camp, especially the rowing and canoeing. I even liked sleeping in a tent, but yes, I was very, very homesick and even cried and was anxious to get home to the safety of my parents. Despite the loneliness, I loved Girl Scout Camp.

Spin the Bottle

So, you can tell by my story so far, that I had discovered boys and my boy "friends" had discovered girls. We were not dating yet. That didn't happen until high school. I did have a 13th birthday party and somehow, with my sister's help no doubt, we played "Spin the Bottle." That was my first kiss. I think it was with Manny or maybe Norman. Norman was two years older, but he came because his father was a "landsman" of my parents. In other words, his father came from Riga,

Latvia. Norman's father would come to our grocery store, especially around Passover, to help my parents out. We met his family, Ed, Norman and Beverly. Norman was the guy who I introduced later to my best friend at college, Betsy, and they eventually married. He was my close friend later in high school, but I met him for the first time at my 8th grade birthday party.

Mind you, the "Spin the Bottle" kisses were far from passionate. They were instead brief and silly, and we'd be laughing all the time. That was the beginning of our time with friends of the opposite sex.

The High School Years

I think I could write an entire book on just those four years of my life. They really opened my world. Those early years were filled with every imaginable emotion—anxiety, depression, exhilaration, confidence building, discovery, exploration, defeats and victories, passion, loneliness, new friendships—all packed into just four short years. I'll share my story in five parts: 1) my life in school, (2) my jobs outside of school, 3) my sorority, 4) my experiences at Sholem Aleichem High School, and 5) my involvement with Young Judaea and my time in Israel.

Perth Amboy High School

The large size of our high school felt intimidating at first. It seemed huge (although it truly wasn't as big as most high schools). I did find my way around the building and registered for the typical college prep classes that most good students took. Freshman and sophomore years felt academically easy, but sophomore biology felt like my first real challenge. Then came junior year chemistry, which brought me my first B—and even a C for one quarter. I still felt like a smart kid, but I began to realize that some students were clearly even smarter, especially Barbara Goldman and Shirley Soos.

I went to school dances, but I never felt like I belonged in the popular crowd. I joined a few school clubs, but I was afraid to try for most. For example, I didn't try out for drama because I didn't think I'd get a part. I didn't join the newspaper because I didn't think I could write well enough. I took a few Baritone lessons but didn't join the band because I didn't think I played well enough.

I did have friends, and I did my homework, and I got good grades. In my junior year I was nominated to the National Honor Society and started to realize that I was a pretty smart high school student after all. It was truly activities outside of our high school that helped me build real confidence, although I had plenty of ups and downs with those as well.

I never expected to go to college until Henrietta Herbert, my guidance counselor, told me that I should go to college. She made a huge difference for me. One Friday, she took me aside at school and said, "Sylvia, you should go to college." She gave me a book of scholarships and said, "Go through these and apply for scholarships and I'll write you letters of reference." I was amazingly flattered. I just didn't think I could do college. That weekend, I went through the whole book and applied for every possible scholarship. Mrs. Herbert wrote me letters of recommendation, and I earned enough scholarship money to cover tuition for all four years and room and board for the first two. I didn't have enough to live on campus for my junior and senior year, so I commuted the last two years. That opportunity to go to college made an amazing difference for me. I am forever grateful to Mrs. Herbert, and I managed to thank her again in person when I received a high school award much later as an adult. She came at age 87 to the award dinner and presented it to me.

My First Jobs

I had helped my parents at the store for many years, so part-time sales seemed like a natural first job. Also, both my sisters had carried part-time jobs successfully. A job opened up for me for Saturdays only, at a children's clothing store and a friend thought I would be perfect. With a combination of excitement and extraordinary fear, I accepted the job. Guess what! They fired me after the first day. They said I was too shy. I think I probably just didn't know what to do at first, and I don't remember their giving me a clue. Nevertheless, that wasn't exactly a confidence builder.

I needed a job. How else could I have any spending money to buy those all- important clothes for high school? I saw a Help Wanted sign at Kresge's 5 & 10- cent store, and I applied and got the job. I hoped I'd be able to keep it. I immediately asked the person just what I was supposed to do, how to do it and what I should be doing when there were no customers around. I smiled at customers when I asked if I could help them and thanked them for their purchases. I trembled when I saw the supervisor watching me, but I plugged ahead, and after six months I even got a small raise. I don't remember how much increase, but it's likely I went from 50 cents an hour to as much as 60 cents an hour.

On weekend evenings I also took up jobs babysitting. The hardest part of babysitting was being afraid at night when I was alone, and the baby was sleeping. I really was a scaredy-cat.

By my junior year of high school, I had moved up to becoming a salesperson for Paramount Clothes, and I even received several raises there. I loved helping teens and even adults find just the clothes they were looking for. I was finally a great success and even worked there in summer while I was in college. Just remember, I was fired from my first job after one day. And incidentally, that did not turn out to be the only time I was fired. I think these days we call that learning "resilience."

My Sorority (DEBS)

In my freshman year I was invited to pledge for the Jewish sorority called DEBS. I think those letters were not initials but DEBS was short for Debutantes. I can't really remember. As part of our pledge period, we were required to attend Friday night Sabbath services at the fancy Reformed Temple in Perth Amboy— a place where, all the wealthier families in the community belonged, but I had never even entered.

The first step in pledging the sorority was to pass through an induction ceremony, where each of us was introduced—one at a time—to all the sorority sisters.

Their mission seemed to be to see how we responded to a large group of silly questions so they could make fun of us. I don't really remember any of the questions, except one. Imagine this:

> The room is full of sophomore through senior girl students, drinking sodas and snacking and laughing. They call in each freshman one at a time, and here comes Sylvia. After a few introductory questions which were straight forward, they came up with, "Could you please define necking?" My first response was, "Did you say necking?" In my head, I said, "What in the world is necking?" Then I responded with pretended confidence, "I believe necking is when a girl and a boy put their necks together."

Can you just hear the uproarious laughter? Of course, mixed with their laughs were comments like "Did you ever do any necking?" and "So that's what necking is!" Then they let me leave the room. I made the cut, but I thought to myself, "I've never been so embarrassed in my life."

I went to Sabbath services every Friday night with my friends, and we partied each week after services at Barbara's house. The girls and guys in our group were very nice and, yes, I did learn what necking was really about.

Sholem Aleichem High School (in New York City)

I was the only student in my Perth Amboy Yiddish School class by graduation from 8th grade. That seems silly, but the teacher had added Hebrew to my Yiddish studies, and I had interesting and devoted Yiddish teachers, both male and female. Gele Schweid was the woman teacher who I adored. She went to study further in Montreal, and I even attended her wedding. The male teacher was Chaver Ruthenberg.

He had survived the Warsaw Ghetto uprising during World War II. He had many interesting stories to tell us.

The next step for me was the weekend Yiddish High School that took place only in New York City. I don't remember the exact location and, of course, I received a scholarship to the school. The only costs were the travel, so I began a weekly train and subway trip to the "City." Yes, that took courage at first, but I became a confident independent traveler and student. I met new friends from the Bronx, Brooklyn, Manhattan, and all over the city. I studied more Yiddish literature and Hebrew and history. What a great confidence builder that was for me. I continued to high school graduation—again a lonely, but significant, ceremony for an immigrant's kid in Perth Amboy, New Jersey.

Young Judaea

The Y program director encouraged me to join Young Judaea in 1949 as a high school freshman. It was a high school age Zionist youth group that was supportive of the new State of Israel, which was founded in 1948. My family friend's son, Norman, was the local president, and he had just returned from a summer program in Israel. We learned about Israel, but most exciting for me, we learned Israeli songs and dances. We formed a dance group and performed for local adult groups—even incorporating Israeli dancing into our rooftop sessions at the Y. Our group traveled to state conferences to join other groups in performance and celebration. We felt like we all had a real sense of purpose, and we had amazing fun.

I also led middle school children in Young Judaea groups and taught them songs and dances. I never had a very good voice, although I always sang with gusto and joy anyway. I even taught the younger children the Israeli songs and dances. I do, with humility, remember some rather negative comments about the "off key" singing of the kids. That person wondered who taught them. I admitted it was I (I never could sing on key anyway). That didn't stop me. I rose to Young Judaea leadership, president at the local level, and vice president at the State level. My boyfriend, Ivan, became president because I didn't think it was right for a girl to take the presidency from a boy. I encouraged Ivan, with great relief, to step into that role instead.

As a leader, I received a scholarship to go to Tel Yehudah, a Young Judaea camp in Asheville, North Carolina. I was no longer homesick and made lots of good friends. I remember seeing the bathroom signs in North Carolina—Whites Only or Negroes Only. That was totally shocking to a girl from the north because we had nothing like that.

Most exciting of my high school experiences was a Young Judaea trip to Israel for six weeks in the summer after my junior year (1952). That was very soon after the founding of the Jewish State in 1948. Part of the time we stayed at a campsite high on a mountain that overlooked Jerusalem. We could see East Jerusalem below. It was still in Arab hands.

In Tel Aviv, we lived with families for a week. Meat was rationed but we could still eat fish and chicken and plenty of vegetables and fruits. I remember our Tel Aviv family managed to get us small steaks using black market prices. Felafel was a real treat when we first tasted it in Tel Aviv.

We also lived and worked on a kibbutz in the desert and picked grapes in the hot sun. We learned about trickle irrigation. We joined with the Kibbutzniks in plenty of Israeli dancing and singing.

On my return from Israel, I remember some interesting thinking and conclusions. I thought that it must be nice to live in a Jewish country where you didn't have any antisemitism and everyone was Jewish. (I think how naïve I was then because poor Israel had so many Arab enemies and there were plenty of wars afterward.) Even now they can't feel safe.

I also remember telling my mother how happy and idealistic the Jewish Kibbutz settlers were, despite their hard work and few material possessions. Her response shocked me. She said, "They are happy because they've never known a better life."

I was annoyed at her, and I said nothing in reply, but in reflection years later, I realized how naïve and optimistic I was and how very wise and realistic she was. Most of those Kibbutzniks had lived through or barely escaped World War II in Europe.

Young Judaea was not extreme in any way as far as religion or Zionism went, but it was perfect for me. I learned a lot of Hebrew and many, many songs and dances. I made wonderful girl and boy friends—all of which together built my confidence and my skills.

My nickname, Simi, came during my high school years. My actual name in Yiddish was Sima, from the Hebrew word Symcha. Symcha means celebration. Or party in Hebrew, so I liked that concept. That was my grandmother's name, as mentioned earlier. Somehow that got shortened to Simi in high school, and that was the name my friends knew. None of my friends from Young Judaea or high school ever thought of me as Sylvia, so Simi I was—even shortened to Sim, for the rest of my days.

When I left high school, I had been going with a nice guy by the name of Sid Horowitz. We decided to break up because we thought we should have a whole new social life in college. Young people were supposed to find their lifelong partners in college.

College Years

Douglass Challenges and Changes

In my freshman year at Douglas College, I felt very lost. I dated quite a few guys, and I had some friends, but I felt like an "immigrant kid." I felt as if I didn't speak correctly and as if I wasn't smart enough. I had been a very smart student in high school. I graduated sixth in my class and got only two Bs in high school.

College was different, and I got mostly Bs at first. I really felt stupid and thought something was wrong with me. I wasn't raised in an upper middle-class environment like many of the other students, and in college, I didn't feel like I truly belonged—either in the Hillel Jewish community or the broader campus community. I felt like I belonged no place. So, I had many ups and downs in college. I thought that maybe I was depressed and even went to the school's psychologist. He didn't seem helpful, so I quit.

How I Met My Future Husband

In my sophomore year of college, a girl in my dormitory named Carolyn, wanted me to meet her boyfriend Barry's roommate—Alfred, nicknamed Bucky. I didn't know about the plan. At Douglass, in those days, no boys could go beyond the living room. You couldn't even let a boy go beyond that front doorway and, of course, we had very strict curfews. We had no co-ed classes. We weren't allowed to take classes at Rutgers and Rutgers guys weren't allowed to take classes with us. So, at the beginning of my sophomore year, when the Rutgers boys would make their rounds through the Douglass campus living rooms to check out the "copies" (that's what they called us at Douglass). My friend Carolyn's boyfriend, Barry, brought this guy named Bucky with him, and Bucky stopped and talked to me.

I knew nothing about this plan and what I remember most is that I was trying to make conversation with this guy, Bucky. I said, "What are your interests?" Bucky said, "You wouldn't be interested in what I'm interested in. I love tropical fish, and I'm an Aggie." Then I said, "Tropical fish. That's really interesting." That seems like a joke now, but we did eventually have many aquariums after we were married. We talked for just a little time and then Bucky left.

It was a setup. A week later at eleven o'clock at night, (long past when we were supposed to be on the phone), Bucky called me. I later learned it took him a lot of courage for him to make that call. He asked me to double date with Carolyn and Barry to go to the Princeton-Rutgers football game. That sounded very cool to me.

So, Carolyn, Barry, Bucky, and I went to the Princeton-Rutgers game. It was a whole day big game date. We even went out to dinner first and then to the game. I remember being very impressed because he brought me an inflatable cushion. I thought that was really special, and we had a fun time. I don't remember who won the game.

After the game, we went out to dinner again. During the conversation, Barry told Carolyn that they would get married right after he graduated from college. Carolyn was only a freshman so I explained to Barry that I didn't think it was the right thing to do because that wouldn't allow Carolyn to finish college. I never would have considered getting married until I finished college, and I didn't think any girl should. Buck often reminded me of how I told his friend off, but I didn't really think I was telling him off. I guess I was a women's "liberator" before the term was ever used. As a result, Barry didn't like me very much because of my unwelcomed advice to Carolyn. After we dropped them off and returned to campus, Buck and I walked around for a while—and he put me through an inquisition of questions about my moral values. I thought, "What is this guy doing?" I guess he wanted to know all about my moral values before he chanced getting involved. We walked for hours. He wanted to know my whole life story.

I didn't think much about Buck until a few weeks later when he called me again. This time we went bicycling together on the Rutgers campus. We enjoyed it, and we started going out regularly. I thought he was a great guy. We studied together. I don't think he would have done much studying without my influence. He liked art and I liked art, and we both liked classical music. We went to the symphony orchestras that came to Rutgers and to lectures, too. We heard Robert Frost reading his poetry, and he bought me a book of his poems that we still have today. We would walk and talk a lot. We really had a lot in common.

Meeting the Parents

Buck came to meet my parents at our home in Perth Amboy. The gift he brought was a record—Beethoven's Ninth Symphony, which we had heard together at a concert. His homemade card set forth a special message. It first showed a book—to represent the Robert Frost collection he had given me—then a record, symbolizing the Beethoven album I had just received. And finally, for the future, a picture of a diamond ring. We were getting serious.

My parents had plenty of questions for him, but most important, they wanted to be sure he was Jewish. Neither he nor I felt very religious in our Judaism, but both of us were clear that we were Jewish.

Gradually, our relationship grew more serious, and by the following November, he invited me to his home in Atlantic City to meet his parents for Thanksgiving dinner. I remember on our drive there, he said, "I hope they like you as much as they like my brother Sig's wife, Barbara." Now that was pressure! I thought, "Oh God, I won't be able to say anything right," and I was afraid to even talk. What his parents said after I left was, "She's so quiet." I guess I thought that was better than saying something wrong that his parents wouldn't like about me.

Plans for the Future

Our relationship gradually evolved. We became good friends together, and I talked about what he would do after college. He wanted to be a farmer. I remember that discussion well.

Buck had worked on a farm one summer for six weeks and, based on that, he decided to become a farmer. He was a Dairy Science major in the School of Agriculture.

I asked him if he had figured out where he would get a farm. He said he thought that maybe his uncle would give him a small farm. Since one of his uncles—Uncle Irving—was critically ill at the time, and his other uncle owned a butcher shop and wasn't exactly wealthy, it didn't make much sense to me. The conclusion seemed to be to think about graduate school. The Rutgers Graduate Program was based at the Dairy Research Farm in Sussex, New Jersey, allowing him to combine his studies with farm life and hands-on work with dairy animals.

Buck talked to his professor and, sure enough, they encouraged him to apply. Although New Jersey was known as The Garden State, there were actually shortages of graduate students in agriculture, so he could easily qualify. Not only did he qualify, but he was offered a $2,000 stipend, tuition free and graduate housing at the outrageously low rent of $15 a month. This looked like a bright future and an opportunity for us to determine if we liked living in a rural area, as well. Engagement and marriage were indeed ahead except for one small problem. I would not marry until I finished college, and I had a full year to go. We solved that problem early. I took courses at summer school and an extra course in the first semester of my senior year. That made it possible for me to graduate a semester early and plan a wedding for mid-January. We would only be apart for one semester.

The Formal Marriage Proposal on the Beach

Buck had a plan. We were visiting his parents again, but it was summer, and we were walking on the beach. Suddenly, my boyfriend got down on his knees, ring in hand, and proposed to me. I burst out laughing. I think that hurt his feelings at the time. I'm sorry, Buck, I didn't mean to, but I just didn't expect that. Of course, I said yes as he slipped the ring on my finger. I was excited. We really were going to plan a wedding.

Chapter 5

Our Early Married Life

Our Wedding

Our wedding was interesting because no one ever heard of such a small wedding. My parents were poor, and they had already borrowed money for my sisters' weddings. There was no way I was going to let them do that for mine. We had 35 people at our wedding.

Buck was late getting to our wedding. I was a little worried. He drove with our sister-in-law, Barbara, who has long since passed away. They missed the correct exit of the New Jersey Parkway. We had a Rabbi and a huppah and a brief ceremony and I was just confused, but it was far from a typical wedding. I just knew we were getting married, and Buck was going back to go to the Dairy Research Farm in Sussex, New Jersey, where he would be a graduate student.

The ceremony was at my sister Frances' home in Lakewood, New Jersey. Then we went to a hotel, and we sat around a dinner table. One of my mother's brothers, Uncle Max, and his wife, Mary, were there from South America and so were our basic family members. There was no dancing or real partying. We had dinner, a few little toasts, and that was it. I guess you don't have to have a large wedding to have a long marriage because we were married for 66 years.

Our Honeymoon

Our honeymoon was also record short. Buck had only a few days before he needed to go back to school. Our quick adventure was a round trip to Vermont to attempt playing in the snow—tobogganing and our first skiing. Vermont was beautiful. Skiing was challenging for me, but Buck did a little better. We were newly together, and unlike many marriages today, we had never lived together before. So "adventure" is the perfect word—it applied just as much to our honeymoon as it did to setting our first home.

Our First Home

Top Floor of a Converted Pig House, Sussex, New Jersey

Our $15 a month rent, first home was above a garage which had been converted from a farm building at the Dairy Research Farm. It had a bedroom, bathroom with a ringer washer in it, a living room and kitchen. I do remember we entertained ourselves by having slide parties at night. Buck was already an amateur photographer, with a collection that included photos from his uranium prospecting days in Colorado, along with family photos from both sides of the family. We had no TV, and we resolved that we wouldn't have TV even after children were born. Our little apartment was about three miles from the main Dairy Research campus. We were completely happy there, though it felt a little lonely for me without any neighbors.

For the first time I had an old car of my own to drive. I had almost no experience driving, and the roads were narrow and rolling. The scenery was beautiful in Sussex County and there was almost no traffic, so it was easy to start finding my way around.

I was accustomed to working. I had part-time jobs since college. I had six credits in education, which allowed me to substitute teach, and there were teacher shortages. I taught various subjects and immediately received a contract to teach in the Sussex schools for the following year. I thought we were all set.

Buck's salary as a graduate assistant was $2,000 a year, but rent was low, and a full cart of groceries cost about $25 or less. We wouldn't have dared to think of going out to eat, and I was comfortable preparing meals and figuring out what both of us liked. I think I remember that our favorite Sunday breakfast was BLT's—bacon, lettuce and tomato—and I'm sure we had plenty of hamburgers, spaghetti and meatballs, and meatloaf throughout the week.

Dairy Research Farm Home #2

At the end of the spring semester, a $15 rent a month new home opened up for us right in the main campus of the Dairy Research Farm. Don't envision a campus--only a farm. Robert and Martha Mather, Buck's major professor, lived in the main home with their children, John and Janet. Sometimes they would invite me to watch TV with them—typically an educational program. Robert Mather had a great and encouraging impact on Buck, while Martha—an educator—was focused on ensuring that her two gifted children were adequately challenged. She taught me a lot and inspired me about gifted children. Their son, John, became a Nobel Prize winner. We remember when he used to go out and look at the stars with his dad and when he borrowed Buck's microscope just because he was motivated to learn.

Our new house was a converted chicken coop with two bedrooms, a kitchen, living room, and a porch above a two-car garage. It had a central heater with a real fire burning. That's where the famous "chinas" originated (drying racks). We would set them around the heater with our clothes, and eventually diapers, drying on them. This is the time when we purchased our first Bendix, used automatic washing machine set in the garage. We still had no dryer. In the summer, I hung the clothes— the first diapers—on the line. In the winter, they dried on the "chinas" set around the stove, and in the spring and fall, the "chinas" moved out to our little porch.

And yes, I was pregnant for the first time, and of course, Ilonna, like all the rest, was unplanned. We did have birth control but no pills, and obviously our birth control wasn't very effective. Most of our friends had between five and nine children, so a four-child family was small for our time.

It was nice being right on the farm because the Mathers and other professors and students were nearby, as were farms with cows and pigs. It was beautiful rolling countryside, and Buck and I were both excited and happy about rural life.

Once I was visibly pregnant, I could no longer substitute teach, but I found a different part-time job. I sold World Book Encyclopedias. I earned a small commission for every set I sold, and along the way, I met many kind, friendly people with children. Most exciting of all—after selling 10 sets, I received a free set for us. (In case you ever wondered where our beautiful encyclopedias came from!) We loved them then and still do. In the days before Siri and Google, World Book was a wonderful sea of knowledge. Interestingly, Grandma Bess had also sold encyclopedias in her younger days, so she was especially delighted at my new part-time endeavor. I was always happy when I could please my mother-in-law.

Ilonna was due in January, and the hills of Sussex County were well-known for their blizzards and snowstorms. This was after all a very first pregnancy, and I was getting close to delivery. A blizzard was predicted, and Ilonna was pushing to arrive. We weren't taking any chances because it was a long hilly drive to the hospital in town. The snow had begun so we were on our way, yes, somewhat early. The doc checked me in and said I'd likely be there overnight before baby was born. Buck went back to study and by nightfall, when he planned to return, all roads were blocked. It was a long, slow birthing, and the hospital had lost all electricity. A nurse held a lantern. In those days we didn't know gender until arrival, but I was delighted when my doctor announced that our little girl was coming into the world. I had read all sorts of books prior to birth on how to give birth without medication for pain, but I was delighted to have all the pain relief my doc could give me. That book advice went out the window, but what a joy to see that beautiful baby. Truly I felt joyous in the morning—so happy and strong that when I needed the restroom, I told the nurse I could get out of bed and go on my own. So much for the few moments of strength—oops—they found me on the floor of the bathroom, crying in pain with blood all over my face.

By the time Buck came to see me in the morning, my face and mouth were bruised, and I looked a mess. Ilonna was asleep in the nursery along with two other little babies born that stormy night. Buck liked to joke about that. He would say he could easily pick out our Ilonna "because she was the only baby reading a book". So, our parenting began and there wasn't any more substitute teaching for that year. Instead, there were diapers everywhere and a "smiling, happy baby".

Bess and Ben came up to visit Ilonna, and I was thankful to receive plenty of advice. Of course, there was Dr. Spock too and I read his book over and over. The Mather kids came over to visit, and I nursed Ilonna happily and wheeled her around the Dairy Research Farm once the weather warmed.

Buck finished his master's degree that year and we made plans for the Air Force years ahead.

The Air Force Conglomeration (As best I remember) Mexico Beach and Training

Buck went into the Air Force as a 2nd Lieutenant since he had taken ROTC as an undergraduate at Rutgers. His master's degree had allowed him to postpone his service obligation and that was happening during the Korean War—fortunate timing. His first training to be an Air Force Navigator began at Pendleton Air Force Base in Pensacola, Florida.

Ilonna was about six months old, and we rented a cottage in a beach subdivision in nearby Mexico Beach. You may recall seeing on the news, just a few years ago, that Mexico Beach was destroyed by a hurricane, but when we were there, it was a lovely little beach community. We were there for a short while. Buck trained and was on base all day, and I basically stayed in the cottage and cared for little Ilonna. I met almost no one. We grocery shopped at the Air Force base and Buck did all the driving. We had only one car, and I was very, very lonely. Fortunately, it was a brief visit, and I at least remember the beauty of the white sand beaches.

We were productive however, because I soon found I was pregnant again with David. The kids were 13 months apart, which means David was conceived in the spring in New Jersey before we moved to Florida. I wasn't feeling very energetic during that hot Florida summer, and it was far too warm to leave our little cottage—through thankfully, it had a window air conditioner.

South Korea for Buck

Buck's next stop was to be a Navigator in South Korea—fortunately, right after the Korean war was over. Mostly, the Air Force was monitoring the border between the two Koreas. Buck always liked to joke about his injury on the "front line" when he served in Korea. After his listener expressed appropriate concern, he'd explain that his injury—a broken nose—happened on the "front line of the volleyball court." That, of course, always brought laughter.

The Air Force offered plenty of recreational opportunities, including the one that allowed Buck to win an award flying his model airplane in a contest in the Philippines. He also brought home some wonderful photographs from his journey and shared slide shows with me and his parents. Our children may find the beautiful photos around the house somewhere when they move me out, but right now I have no idea where they are. I'm sure they will enjoy viewing them.

Living Back with Parents

In the fall of 1958, I moved back home to Perth Amboy and lived with my parents for about five months. Since pregnant women weren't allowed to teach—and Ilonna needed plenty of care—I used that one semester of free babysitting from Grandma Reva to try returning to graduate school at Rutgers. I was planning to do graduate work in Sociology and could drive into New Brunswick twice a week to take one course. I was still deciding whether Sociology or Social Work would be my final career direction, rather than teaching. The semester went quickly, and my next planned step was to move to Atlantic City, where I planned to give birth to David.

My parents had no car, and they were immigrants. I'm not sure whether my mother already had her cancer colostomy surgery by then, so her health may have also been a major concern. I had less confidence in my mom's ability to help me with the plan for baby delivery and managing Ilonna. I had total confidence in Grandmom Bess, and she was eager and enthusiastic about helping me.

In Atlantic City with Bess and Ben

The first babies usually take longer to deliver, but our second baby, David, shocked us and came very quickly, likely since he came only 13 months later. Bess always joked that she "didn't even have time for the tea kettle to boil" before they called her back to the hospital—because David had been delivered. She came driving right back to see our beautiful newborn little David.

David's first months were at my in-laws' home. Grandmom Bess was a very kind, caring, confident, strong lady, and I was an anxious, lacking in confidence, very young woman (23). She told me what to do, as well as all the things that I did wrong, and she tried to be helpful. When we lived with her, I had little confidence and was somewhat depressed. I remember taking one anti-depressant pill prescribed by Bess's doctor friend, but then I decided to manage without it—and I did, despite my normal anxiety and loneliness.

Grandmom later said it was her favorite time in life. She became a very happy grandma and enjoyed those young grandchildren. I felt like everything I did was wrong, but I loved my in-laws, and Grandmom Bess helped me and taught me a lot. For most, grandparenting is a special time—and they were no exception. They were wonderful and absolutely delighted with both Ilonna and baby David.

By that time Ilonna was already loving books that I read to her. She was also very sweet with her little baby brother though she wasn't much older than he was.

Off to Texas to a Trailer Home

Buck returned from Korea where he had been promoted to First Lieutenant, and now it was time to get ready for promotion to Captain. Officer training took us to San Antonio, Texas for six weeks. Now imagine this. We rented a little trailer and lived in a beautiful park in central San Antonio. I remember I could take our two babies for walks along the river, and during the day I would read to both of them. My biggest problem was that energetic "little Dadee" needed very little sleep, and it was hard to keep up with his incredible pace.

And Back to Panama City

Buck was called back to Tyndall Air Force Base, and we rented a nice three-bedroom home in Panama City while he completed his last year as Captain in the Air Force. We had two cars so I could get around. Buck was busy training other servicemen, and I was very busy taking care of the babies. I remember a double- decker stroller, with Ilonna on the upper level. We could even walk to Piggly Wiggly and pick up a few groceries that fit in the attached basket. The weather was mild and beautiful. I recall we also did some walking as a family on the beautiful white sand beaches of Panama City.

Ilonna was an easy toddler, but David kept me busy chasing after him. He needed very little sleep. I was always thankful that I could manage a nap while he and Ilonna both napped in the afternoon or at least played quietly alone.

The Rutgers, New Brunswick Circle

When Buck returned to school, the Agriculture school arranged for him to take course work at the New Brunswick campus for a year.

Rutgers had reserved two large circles of small homes in New Brunswick for graduate students' families and faculty. The area was a few miles from the main campus and the centers of the circles were grassed in for family recreational use.

There were many young families, and I easily made friends with other women who had babies or young children. That was nice for our toddlers, too, and much easier for me. I do remember (just once) that little David wandered far away into the second circle, including crossing a road alone—all before I found him. That was scary. I resolved to never let him out of my sight again.

It was here that we met our good friends, Barbara and Christopher Rose-Innes and their two sons. The older boy, Nicholas, was a year older than Ilonna and they played together a lot. The younger child, Alexander (Zander), was retarded and autistic—a Downs Syndrome child. We stayed best friends with the family that year and continued to be friends for many years afterward. We visited them in England, and they came back and visited us in Key Largo. We continued exchanging Christmas messages until a year ago. I wonder if they are still alive.

They were in their early 90's when I last heard from them.

Oh yes—we had no automatic dryer yet in New Brunswick. I remember hanging the baby diapers on the line outside to dry.

Gingerbread Castle Road—Sussex, New Jersey

Buck's last year of graduate school was heavily directed toward his research dissertation. All Dairy Research Farm homes were already taken by other students, but the school helped us find a four-bedroom small home near the farm in Hamburg, New Jersey, on Gingerbread Castle Road. Yes, it had a real Gingerbread Castle tourist attraction right near us and we visited several times. We had a few friends in the neighborhood with toddlers our children's ages, and it was during that time that I realized that I realized just how verbal Ilonna and David were. David, at two years of age, talked like a "little talking machine," and Ilonna, at age three, knew her letters and numbers and was beginning to read words. I found some workbooks for Kindergarteners, and she loved completing the pages.

Buck was in graduate school for only a total of four years for his PhD and he was a wonderful student. He really loved his work and was a very creative successful graduate student. His major professor was Robert Mather. Robert and his wife, Martha, had great inspiring impacts on us both.

Robert (Bob) Mather mentored Buck in his research and he had forever appreciated that. Both were wonderful role models for good parenting. For example, we remember when Bob would take his son, John, out with a telescope to study the sky. John borrowed Buck's microscope so his dad could help him discover how to use it. Martha shared with me all the efforts she made to ensure that John and Janet were challenged in school. She explained how important meaningful learning was for gifted students—and how poorly most schools addressed these issues. She was a role model for my future concerns for our children and for my career as well. Little did we, or they, know then that John would become a Nobel Prize winner. They were just two smart kids who needed special educational opportunities. Their parents were also very careful about television viewing, which likely influenced our own decision never to have a television in our home while raising our children.

Then Buck's PhD graduation came. Bess and Ben came to join us and the kids in New Brunswick when Buck was awarded his PhD Diploma, and the real world of work was about to begin for us.

CHAPTER 6

Buck's First Job— Millington, New Jersey

When Buck got his PhD, he searched for jobs in his major, Dairy Genetics. There wasn't a single job in the whole country, not even one single opening. There was nothing even to apply to. However, biostatisticians were in short supply, so instead, he applied for a job with Maxwell House Coffee, where he conducted statistical analysis of data related to their first freeze-dried coffee. I remember when he got that job. As he drove in the driveway, I called to him, "Buck, Maxwell House Coffee called." He took that job, and we moved to Millington, New Jersey, and rented a house there.

I was definitely a stay-at-home mom, but very busy with Ilonna, age four and a half and David, age three. A preschool might have worked for both, but we had no money to pay for preschool. At that point Ilonna was reading fluently at about the 3rd grade level. After I read to the children, I would hear her reading the books back from her crib even when she was three. It seemed logical for her to go to kindergarten, but her birthday was two weeks past the deadline for admission.

I bravely called the school principal to make an appointment to request early entrance to school. I remember trembling as I talked to him about the issue of both her high reading level and her strong abilities of counting, adding and subtracting. He listened impatiently and cut into my conversation quickly. He simply said, "absolutely no" and further advised me to "stop pressuring" my child. The tears leaked from my eyes, and he calmly ended the conversation with advising me to call the phone number of a private kindergarten. He told me the school would accept her the following year into first grade only if the private kindergarten advised it.

So, I was off to the private Kindergarten the next day. They were happy to accept her, but the tuition seemed impossible. They asked me about my background and offered me a job as an enrichment teacher for their gifted students in exchange for Ilonna's tuition. I agreed to work two mornings a week while David attended their preschool, and my work would pay for both children's schooling. What a great opportunity for me and for the children. It worked well for all of us for a very short time—approximately one school year.

Then Buck realized that being a Maxwell House Coffee statistician was not the career for him.

CHAPTER 7

Buck's Second Job—In Buffalo and Our Many Homes During That Time

While still in New Jersey, Buck received a phone call from Roswell Park in Buffalo, New York. It was a cancer research institute, and they needed a biostatistician. He had applied for the job earlier but had not heard anything so when he finally heard from them, he knew this was an important opportunity. He interviewed and was accepted for the position.

The field of biostatistics was mainly created in agriculture. Buck's strong background in statistics opened the door to an entirely new career—conducting biostatistical research in the medical field. It was also the beginning of the entire field of Epidemiology. We were in Buffalo for three years while he was at Roswell Park and where he officially became a biostatistician and epidemiologist. It really changed his life and the way he looked at research, and he absolutely loved doing the research. He was good and very creative.

In my work one of the most interesting kinds of kids that I work with are gifted kids who "march to the beat of a different drummer." They're highly creative but often struggle within structure because their very persona is one of being different—unusual, and out of step with others. That's the classic person that Buck was as a child. When he viewed a problem, he always saw what was different about it and how to change it. By the time he went to Buffalo, he had learned the rigor that he needed for statistics, and excellent research skills, as well.

Buffalo Adventure—Living in NJ with Vivian and Irv's Family

Our move to the Buffalo area was complicated. Our hope was eventually to move to a farm so Buck could fulfill his dream of living an agricultural life. But we knew that would take time, research, and a better understanding of the area—so we decided to rent a house first. We found a lovely little home in a subdivision on Grand Island, New York—a quick drive to work for Buck and a lovely community right near a beautiful school.

Unfortunately, health problems had multiplied for my parents. My dad's Parkinson's Disease had become very extreme, and my mother's colostomy had not solved her cancer problem. Cancer had returned. Both parents were hospitalized at Roosevelt Hospital in New Jersey. My mother's cancer was considered terminal, although in those days, doctors never told patients when their cases were terminal. She had hope but we knew better. I wanted to be near her in her final weeks, and we knew that would not be a long time. So, Buck stayed at the rental house, and I and the kids moved in with Viv and Irv and their kids for several months. We visited Mom and Dad at the hospital daily.

Ilonna and David played with Ira, now Jay and Matt, and Buck would visit us every two weeks for the weekend.

I remember how wonderful Viv and Irv were to me during that time. We were all so worried about our parents, but we knew Mom (Reva) didn't have long.

I also remember that Aunt Vivian was a heavy smoker during that time. The research on lung cancer was not yet published, and there were always cigarette butts and smoke around. But Aunt Vivian and Aunt Frances stopped smoking entirely after the research was published.

On one of the weekends that Buck visited, the doctor informed us that Mom was dying, and it was time to take her off oxygen. We had to give him permission. My mom likely knew. She said in Yiddish,

"Me bagrupt mir tsu schnell"—which translated means, "They're burying me too soon." She was not ready to give up but there was no hope for recovery, and so sadly we watched her pass away. Our dad was in the room with us and was aware and in tears, as was I, when she took her last breath—at age 60. Although I felt very sad, I actually thought she was old at the time.

Our dad outlived our mom for four more years at the hospital, and I would come and visit him from Buffalo from time to time. My sisters would visit him often, but Parkinson's was a terrible disease for him to live with.

Grand Island, New York

We moved into our lovely little home in Grand Island and our children quickly found friends to play with. If you're counting, this was move 11. I think David's little friend was named Patty. Since Ilonna had completed kindergarten, the Grand Island school accepted her into 1st grade. By that time Ilonna was reading chapter books on her own. However, I was afraid to even talk to the teacher because I had been terrified by the earlier principal in New Jersey.

Soon after school started, I was in the local supermarket and Ilonna's 1st grade teacher saw me and stopped me to talk. Her words surprised and delighted me. She said, "Your daughter is so well adjusted and delightful, but I'm having the school psychologist test her because I don't think she's being challenged enough in my class." Next, I was called to meet with the school psychologist, and he said, "Ilonna's very well socially adjusted, but she needs more reading and more math challenges. We decided to send her up to second grade for reading, and we'll give her extra enrichment work in math in first grade so she stays challenged. She gets along well with children, and she doesn't have any problems." I was happy, but I also remember thinking to myself, "I want a job like that school psychologist someday." That meeting truly inspired my wanting to become a psychologist specializing in gifted children.

Of course, I couldn't do that yet. My major was sociology, and while I was in Buffalo, I completed three graduate school credits in sociology. I did a research paper on "The Childhoods of Successful Musicians and Artists" as part of my class research. So, even then, I was interested in the characteristics of gifted children. More about my change in career direction later.

We were happy in Grand Island. I think that's where Ilonna learned to ride a little bicycle, and David seemed to settle into a nice, less mischievous routine as he started in kindergarten. His adjustment to school went wonderfully.

I also remember that we were very near Niagara Falls and visited multiple times. They were so beautiful.

Wilson, New York—Shadigee Road (Move #12)

Buck's dream had always been to live on a farm. He now had a perfect job—he loved his new work, and he had interesting colleagues. He was doing cancer research and was teaching a course in Biostatics at the Medical College. We finally found a dream farm in Wilson, New York— just north of Buffalo. It was a rather old house that needed remodeling. It had been an apple orchard, and its' trees still had plenty of apple blossoms and apples for sauce and pies. We invited Buck's colleagues to our home for summer parties, and our friends Bob and Flo Gibson, along with their five children, joined us for help with remodeling, food and fun.

Summers were beautiful. Winters were also incredible with more snow than any of us could have imagined. I can remember it being piled high out our window with a Volkswagen stuck at the top of the snow pile. We also had lots of school closings because of snow.

David loved 1st grade year with Mrs. Pease, and that high-energy little boy had not a single disruptive problem. I do remember his teacher commenting on his "rushing through his work to be the first one done," but he always did good work. There was no need to worry about skipping grades for him and plenty of happy playmates at the playground playing sports.

Ilonna's school placement was a different problem. She had completed second- grade reading and more than first-grade math, but the Wilson School couldn't imagine how to accommodate her being in two different grades. Either she would have to repeat the same book and workbooks in 2nd grade or skip to 3rd grade math. That was an easy decision for us, so it appeared her 2nd grade skip was absolutely necessary. The principal walked us over to meet her third- grade teacher, who looked at Ilonna strangely and, within her hearing, said aloud "I don't see how she can make it; she's so small."

Two weeks later, her teacher reassured me and indicated Ilonna had made a great adjustment and had even made friends. We had to remind Ilonna frequently that "good things can come in small packages." She had lovely 3rd and 4th grade years before it was time to move schools again.

A memory for Ilonna and David from our Wilson home may be their favorite game when Daddy came home from work. If they could be very quiet and play nicely while Mommy and Daddy had their dinner, Daddy would play "Huckle Buckle Beanstalk" with them. He would hide candies and lids from jelly jars around the house, then call to the kids 'Look high and look low'. As they looked for them, he would tell them if they were "hot" or "cold" and when they found them, they would call out "Huckle Buckle Beanstalk." They absolutely loved the game and that fun continued for a few years.

While we lived in Wilson, our little Eric joined the family. I was terrified—after David's rapid birth—that I wouldn't make it to the hospital on time, so I convinced the doctor to induce Eric's birth right around his due date. Eric's birth was lovely and by then I was an experienced mom.

Bess and Ben came to visit us and our new baby, of course. That was the beginning of yearly August visits for so many of Eric's birthday parties. We have another pleasant memory of Eric's early days. Bess thought it might be nice if Bubbie (Anna Keyser) could come up and stay with us for a few weeks. I can picture her now giving Eric his bottle and rocking him from time to time. It was the first and last of Bubbie's visits to us, but it was very special. She was in her late 80s by then, and she soon passed away at 91.

SUNY at Buffalo and then to Wisconsin

I am absolutely uncertain of how I managed to go back to school, part-time, to continue my graduate work. I know I was determined to have a real career. I think because Buck was teaching at SUNY (State University of New York), I could attend tuition free. I know I loved my course work in Sociology, but I took only one course a semester and then it was time to move again.

I'm not sure how the Medical College of Wisconsin got Buck's application, but they clearly wanted him to teach biostatistics and epidemiology—as a real "Assistant Professor." It was an opportunity too spectacular to turn down.

Although we loved Buffalo in spring and summer, the amazing winter blizzards and long dark days would absolutely not be missed. As I recall, the sun hid from view from October to April. We were excited and ready to move to Wisconsin that summer. By then, we had accumulated plenty of furniture, toys, clothes and cars, so this would not be a small or easy move.

CHAPTER 8

The Move to Wisconsin in Four Movements

As with all moves, we knew we would not likely find a farm, our preferred home, at first. Buck and I went up for a quick weekend to find a rental property for start-up. We were intrigued with the Native American place names—like Oconomowoc, Waukesha, Nagawicka—that we hilariously mispronounced at first. We laughed as help from locals corrected our silly attempts. Of course, a farm was not so easy to find, but amazingly, we found a beautiful rental home on a lake—Lake Nagawicka right at the Sawyer Road exit of the freeway. We were excited about the home, and now imagine this:

Buck drove a U-Haul truck and David and a few cats were up front with them. I drove a car—trailing another car— all the way from Buffalo, New York to Delafield, Wisconsin with Ilonna and Eric in a car seat. We transported all Buck's handmade furniture: a sofa, a round table and four chairs, two bureaus, the twin beds (of course), bookcases, boxes, a crib, and plenty of baby furniture and toys. I think we lost a cat along the way. I believe we drove all through the night because I can't remember stopping anywhere. By then Ilonna was nine and David was eight, so they could actually help us move things. It never even occurred to us to hire professional movers. We always moved ourselves.

Lower Nashota Lake

For one beautiful year, we lived on Lower Nashota Lake. While we lived on the lake, Buck bought a 16' wooden boat with a very small, old outboard motor, and he would take David fishing for Blue Gills.

We had one year at Summit School with "Mr. Kohler" as principal and it was spectacular. He immediately had Ilonna and David tested, explaining that Ilonna was highly gifted but could stay in fourth grade with appropriate acceleration through grouping. David, he said, would be sufficiently challenged in his high-ability group. It took a little time for Ilonna to make friends, but 2nd grade David easily found friends playing kickball and marbles on the playground. I'm not sure how I managed baby Eric, but I did substitute teaching one or two days a week in Summit, and I enjoyed it. I also bicycled around the lake when Buck was at home on weekends. He was very busy in his new career during the week. I was busy caring for kids and searching for a farm.

Teaching biostatics as an assistant professor at a medical school was challenging and exciting for Buck. The class makeup was 99% white males with only two women in the class, both of whom were nuns. The school at the time was still known as Marquette Medical School but was changed to the Medical College of Wisconsin soon afterward, and women and minorities trickled into classes slowly.

Our First Wisconsin Farm

Our whole family was excited when we found a small farm. It was right off Highway 16 on Hustisford Road. It had some fruit trees, a big barn with a dad- made barn swing and even a small, wooded area for very short hikes. It brought us into the Watertown School District—a disappointing change from the Oconomowoc District— but once we moved to this farm, we were determined not to change school districts again. At this point, I believe I calculated that Ilonna had moved at least 27 times. She started 5th grade at Webster and David started 3rd grade. As usual, the kids made friends— David, thanks to his love of sports, had no problems with transitions, while

Ilonna often struggled at first but usually found a few close friends over time. As for Ilonna, there were always subject accelerations that needed to be made. The Watertown schools clearly weren't invested in "gifted" education— principals looked at me blankly when I explained the work was too easy for my children.

Eric, too, was soon ready for school. He went to Gingerbread Nursery School—they didn't call them pre-schools in those days. As a three-year-old, he went two half-days a week and at age four he went three half-days a week.

I did substitute teaching in everything from kindergarten through high school. I remember trying to teach high school Spanish without ever having taken a course in Spanish. I had to keep the kids busy working, but I wasn't happy with substituting as a final career. Substituting kept me connected to students and confirmed that I definitely wanted to work with children. But with three of my own at home, I couldn't take a full-time job. I was happy to go back to teaching part-time.

Our house needed remodeling because it was originally a two-family house. We used the downstairs bedroom as a study for Buck and had our bedrooms all upstairs. Ilonna's room had been the kitchen, so it came with built-in counter and drawer space for her clothes—plus a lovely outdoor balcony with a beautiful view. David had a bedroom to himself until Sara was born and then Eric joined him in his room. Baby Sara, born in Watertown, moved into a small bedroom near ours.

The kids started some real farm work by planting trees. Of course, there was a basketball hoop and a field to kick the ball around. I can easily remember David teaching his little brother how to play basketball, football and baseball. Ilonna did some of the cooking with mommy and plenty of reading. She absolutely loved books and was a superb student. I didn't think she ever, ever earned less than an A on any assignment. Although I continued to hear that David was an excellent student, he continued to occasionally make careless mistakes in his hurry to finish his work.

The kids all loved the barn swing and Buck would push them very high.

Ilonna loved to help with little Eric, too. It was around that time we heard Eric jabbering in the back seat of the car, saying, "My name used to be Schmata-too-ta, and then I changed to Eric"—his own playful take on hearing how Rimkuvsky had been changed to Rimm by his daddy's family.

After Sara was born, our little house was feeling crowded, so I began looking around for a farm that had a little larger house. I was determined that it would be in the Watertown School District. The kids had already been to too many school districts.

Farm #2—Apple Bapple Orchard (Move #15)

In my fun search, I discovered a 160-acre farm north of Watertown that seemed qualified for a long time stay. The house needed some work, but it had full potential for our family. It was in the same Watertown School District. We built a primary bedroom on the main floor. Upstairs there were three bedrooms and there was a small bedroom for Sara on the first floor that became a laundry room when Ilonna went to college. I can't quite remember if the boys shared a bedroom. The house was located down a half-mile dirt road, so we didn't have to worry about traffic near our home. The kids—and our dogs, cats, and kittens—could run freely and play in the yard, barns, and surrounding buildings. It even had school bus pick up right at the house. It had hay fields and woods and a potential pond that we eventually had dug out for swimming and ice skating. Buck came and checked it out and loved it. Over time, we bought two neighboring farms and expanded our home and land—eventually becoming Apple Bapple Orchards and Educational Assessment Service, Inc. All that took place over a period of 26 years and was the beautiful farm home where our children grew up.

After two years Buck and David started baling hay and after three or four years started planting apple trees. We eventually planted an apple orchard on the farm, and our kids developed a wonderful work ethic and appreciation of nature.

There was absolutely no television in our home, which was quite amazing for our time. Instead, our kids would read, make things, or do things like hike and bike. They played basketball at their hoop outside, and they would typically have friends over one day each weekend. They all belonged to Girl Scouts or Boy Scouts and had many scout activities. David earned his Eagle Scout rank at age 13. They also all played musical instruments and played in the school bands and orchestras. Eric did drama as well. They all had plenty of healthy extracurricular activities, which gave them meaningful opportunities to explore their interests and build social connections.

More About the Orchard

There is a lot more to say about our orchard. Our farm days in Wilson, New York, got us started with the love of apple trees, and Buck's idea for the orchard started with only a few dozen trees. Then he gradually became an absolute apple tree connoisseur. He learned everything there was to know about apples—different varieties, rootstocks, grafting techniques, and mouse guards to protect the trees from the deer. He installed trickle irrigation to support their growth and planted enough types that, eventually, we could boast about 100 different varieties—ripening from mid-summer all the way through October.

Everyone helped with the planting. Even little Sara assisted by dropping fertilizer packets in each hole. Scout troops had planting camp outs and weekend overnight friends pitched in and planted too.

Over time, we cultivated a small forest of other trees including, over 5,000 evergreens. Each year, our orchard grew larger—eventually reaching over 10,000 trees. We needed plenty of pickers and we needed coolers to store apples. Buck and the boys built coolers in the barn. There were enough apples so we could make our own cider. We purchased a cider press, first a small one, then a larger one. We cooked lots of applesauce and together we baked many favorite apple pies. Eventually we had so much produce that we hired our neighbor,

Mrs. Rice, to sell apples at the barn. Our cousin, Scott Taber, along with others ran the entire operation for a few years—managing the picking, sales, and all the weeding that had to be done. Yes, at that point, we needed an apple orchard manager.

We also featured orchard rides where Buck drove the tractor pulling the farm wagon of guests. The Orchard Guru (Buck) would lecture on rootstocks and the history of various apples. I would co-host those wagon trips and sit on the wagon with the guests, and they were really fun. School, scout and family groups joined us on those fun rides.

We also enjoyed Apple Bapple Orchard sales at the Saturday market at the Madison Square. Each of the young adult kids who were at school in Madison had their turns helping us at our apple stand. They certainly can remember their mother singing out, "Best apple cider on the square—right here." And then there were those after-market lunches together at Ella's Deli.

If you've forgotten about the origin of our Apple Bapple Orchard name, it came because when our children were little, I used to rhyme things all the time—like "warm as a form", "cold as a bold" or "silly as a billy"—thus, the name Apple Bapple naturally emerged. We tried to get the county to name our road Apple Bapple Road. They did it at least halfway—they named it Apple Road, a clear entrance way to our orchard.

In case you think we made money on our apple sales—unfortunately, we did not. We didn't even break-even but no regrets. There was so much love wrapped up in growing apples, sharing apple pies, and watching the amazing orchard that emerged from our joint family adventure. It was just wonderful!

There was only one very sad day that I even hate to talk about. Our beautiful Apple Bapple Orchard sign was out on Highway M to direct visitors to make the turn on Apple Road. One morning, we discovered that swastikas had been painted over our sign—a painful reminder that antisemitism still exists and that we must never forget it's presence.

Family Photos

Sylvia's Mom, Dad, and sisters

Sylvia's Dad and uncles

Family Passover Seder (Sylvai is the baby)

Sylvia and sisters, Frances and Vivian

Sylvia and sisters, Francies and Vivian

Family Vacation

Family at Wisconsin Farm

Sylvia and Katie Couric from the Today Show

CHAPTER 9

More About Wisconsin School Days Again (Early)

Ilonna and David were able to attend Webster School despite the move. They had settled in and made friends. Eric began attending Gingerbread Nursery School three half-days a week and of course Sara, born in Watertown, was still a toddler. When we moved to Watertown, I immediately started substitute teaching in the schools and learned a lot about them—both the good and the not- so-good. I thought there should be opportunities for gifted students, but I liked the general teacher and student attitudes at the school. We had found a really nice living environment for our children.

Then personal opportunities began to emerge: (1) I could join with other parents to form a parent association for gifted children and become active in state and national organizations for gifted education; (2) I could run for election to the school board and work to improve educational opportunities for all students; and (3) I could finally return to school and prepare for a meaningful career of my own.

Gifted Politics and School Board Days

Gifted education was growing on the national scene and in Wisconsin, as well. I joined a small group of parents and teachers involved in the Wisconsin Association for Gifted and Talented Children, and they encouraged me to start a local parenting group in Watertown. I found a wonderful friend, March Schultz, who was indeed interested and shared my concerns. Her daughter had also skipped two grades and teachers constantly compared Ilonna to "the Schultz girl." Not only that, her son's test scores were highly gifted and creative, but they didn't need grade skips. We had much in common and in an alliance in forming a parent group for gifted and creative children. We soon had a new parent group going. We wrote to our legislators and went into Madison to speak up requesting gifted legislation. We managed to get some laws enacted and our Watertown School District was taking notice.

If I ran for the Watertown Board of Education, perhaps we could even improve the schools. Not many people knew me—how would I ever get elected? Here I was a Jewish mother in a mainly German community with plenty of antisemitism—who would vote for me? Worst of all I was a woman, and our Board of Education had never ever had a woman board member. At least I was not entirely alone. Jeanne Reed, the wife of Dr. Bill Reed, also decided to run for the Board at the same time. People referred to us as "the women" running for the Board.

I needed a cause—but good education for gifted kids and all kids would not be enough to set me apart. Then I got my break. The School Board decided they wanted to build a brand-new school and that could mean plenty of taxpayer money. Very few citizens wanted to pay increased taxes, nor did we. An idea came to me almost as a dream. What about if they built some additions to two or three schools. That would cost much less and make for the space needed for students. A campaign that included a money saver encouraged me to run for election.

March Schultz and my friends, John and Mary Wagner, helped support my cause. The idea caught on.

With much trembling and nervousness, I spoke to political crowds and even debated to audiences. And guess what—I actually won the election and served for two terms. I even had the opportunity to help select a superintendent who believed in gifted education. I remember there were twenty male applicants for the position but not a single woman.

I loved serving on the Board except at teacher salary negotiation time. That became quite hostile. I helped the Watertown schools improve their educational opportunities for all students, at least a little bit. I have fond memories of our teachers and schools, and our children thrived in the school environment.

Our Good Friends in Wisconsin

Over the 26 years in Wisconsin, we had many good friends and no doubt I'll forget a few, but I'd like to try and remember. Friends were very important in our lives.

Babs and Mort Bortin were undoubtedly our closest professional and personal friends. Buck worked very closely with Mort related to the biostatistics in his important cancer research. Since other staff members were also involved, the relationship extended to staff parties and conference trips, where they often presented together. The Bortins were somewhat older than we were and, in many ways, mentors too. For example, Babs was the only woman that I knew that developed a professional career while her children were still at home. She was an educational evaluator for some of the Milwaukee Public school programs. She inspired me to follow a similar path, and sometime later, I founded Educational Assessment Service, Inc. With Buck's statistical expertise—and his unwavering moral support—we evaluated school programs in Minneapolis St. Paul, and several other districts as well.

Mort and Babs were such talented people in so many ways, including art and music. Mort could sit at the piano and play everything or anything without looking at music. We enjoyed so many lovely parties at their home.

Unfortunately, both Mort and Babs were heavy smokers, and they passed away at far too young ages—both in their early 70's. Their son was a slumped glass artist, and they gifted us some of his beautiful work.

We also developed a very close friendship with Art and Ellen Hartz and their two daughters. Art worked closely with Buck on epidemiological research—including studies on alcohol and its potential protective effects against heart disease—as well as other topics. We joined their family from time to time for Shabbat family dinners, and they visited our farm occasionally.

The Wagners, John and Mary and their family were likely among our closest friends in Watertown. John was our veterinarian—he gave our dogs and cats their vaccinations and made farm visits. We often stopped by their home to share a drink and some good cheer. They had nine children, and John had been an officer in the Army, so meals often had a good-natured military style. Some of their kids were also friends with our kids, and I convinced Mary eventually to at least join me for one term on the Watertown Board of Education.

I met Carol Himmerich when Eric and her son, Dan, were in preschool together. Carol and I became very close friends. Dan was a very gifted child and Carol's husband, Fred, was an Episcopal Priest. Their kids were Rebecca, Dan, Elizabeth, Sarah and Catherine. I stopped at their home frequently because Dan and Eric, and later Sarah and Sara, became good friends.

Many years later Dan met me in Hong Kong where he was working and was giving talks, and we toured a bit together. Of course, I was there for a short visit, but he worked there for quite a while. Also, Elizabeth, as an adult, came to see me about her very gifted daughter who eventually went to University Lake School and is likely in college by now. Sadly, Carol Himmerich became ill with cancer and passed away far too young—in her late 60's or early 70's. But she and I shared a wonderful friendship that lasted many years.

Peggy and Pete Sheldon were close friends who shared our love of music.

We went to the Milwaukee Symphony concert series together and usually to dinner too. Pete worked at the Medical College of Wisconsin and Peggy was a Social Worker. We all loved music. Unfortunately, Pete died of a heart attack, and although Peggy was in touch a few times afterwards, she moved away to be closer to her children.

The Blumensons, Les and Edith, visited our farm several times. Les worked with Buck. They had a daughter, Amy—about the same age as Eric. Although we weren't close for long—since they divorced and lost touch—I've continued to use Edith's chicken recipe, made with ginger and garlic powder—yummy, yummy.

Barbara Lorman and her family also became close friends. They were almost the only Jewish family that we knew in the area. Barbara's husband was in the State Assembly when he died of a heart attack. They convinced Barbara to run for the seat, and she stayed in the position for several terms. Her family, a daughter and two sons, Bill and David, joined us for Passover Seder several times. It was also Barbara who arranged for my appointment to the Wisconsin Psychology Licensing Board—an experience that proved to be both meaningful and fascinating for me. I'm still in touch with Barbara Lorman, and I visited with her in Wisconsin just last year.

Bob Truit's family also visited us at the farm. They had five daughters. I do remember that they were hoping for that fifth one to be a son. We were all at a professional dinner together when the announcement came that his wife had given birth to another girl. In those days we didn't know the gender of a child until it was delivered. There was a strange silence at the announcement and only after a disappointing deep breath came the more familiar joyous congratulations. Sara reminded me that the Truit family came to visit us at the apple orchard and helped us make cider using our first small apple press. It was a family adventure.

Elaine and Steve Kraut were very good friends we made later in Wisconsin. I met Elaine when I served on the Board of University Lake School when Sara attended that school, and their children, Heidi, Bob and Tim, also attended. I served on the Board a very short time, but we became long-time friends with the Krauts. We visited each other often and traveled together, too. A particularly memorable cruise to Italy cemented a life-long friendship. Although we saw them less often after selling the farm, we.ve remained in touch ever since.

Our Children's School Days Again

I can't say for certain whether my serving on the Board brought gifted programming to Watertown schools or whether the times were changing. However, the gifted enrichment program and subject acceleration were helpful for all our children.

For Ilonna, the school allows her to attend college courses at the University of Wisconsin while still in high school. She had earned enough credits to graduate two years early—and she did.

David was in a high math group and was in gifted enrichment. He did take a college class in psychology while still in high school but was our only child who graduated at the appropriate age. He had excellent grades, a very active school social life and showed true leadership in his class. (I think he was president of the student council.)

Eric was also in gifted programming and accelerated a full year in math all through school. He completed the highest math and science offered during his junior year in high school. He also had a very good social life, was in drama and played tennis, too. He enrolled full-time at the University of Wisconsin after his junior year but graduated from high school with his class, having completed a full year of college in the meantime.

Sara was involved in gifted programming all through school and in high ability groups but needed no grade skips. After she completed 9th grade in middle school, we explored her entering University Lake School (ULS). I had worked with ULS through my clinical work, and it seemed like a potentially very enriching experience. She attended for two years, and it turned out to be a mixed experience. I can credit ULS for giving her excellent writing skills. She had a very special English teacher. She also enjoyed some different friendships and plenty of extracurricular activities. I'm not sure she was entirely happy with the school, and financially it was a lot for us to manage. We felt she was ready for UW-Madison and, since she had enough credits to graduate after her junior year, she did.

All four of our children enjoyed being students at UW-Madison. Of course, they had their ups and downs with both academics and friendships. They had amazing opportunities to work with professors in various laboratory settings, and those experiences proved crucial in opening doors to a range of graduate and medical school programs.

Back to School at UW-Madison

My new career direction developed out of my children's needs and experiences. As you may recall, I mentioned that Martha Mather had been an important influence on me. When we lived at the Dairy Research Farm, she had explained frequently that public schools must address the needs of gifted students. She had made many frustrating efforts for her own children; now it was my turn, both as a professional and as a parent.

This was my third attempt at returning to school and I remember thinking, "Three strikes and you're out." I was determined this time to complete my master's degree and become a school psychologist. I could only enroll part time with three children. Sara was born in Wisconsin a year after I started graduate school. She later joked that she had been to graduate school "in utero." "Mommy" Joyce Koser took care of her when I went to class twice a week. Part time in-state tuition was reasonable in those days. Furthermore, as a part timer, I could escape taking the Graduate Record Exam. The thought of taking the exam terrified me because I was already 32 and had been far from the classroom for many years. I enrolled in two classes each semester in the School Psychology program.

As I continued, I told my major professor, Dr. John Giebink, that I wanted to specialize in gifted children. He responded with, "Gifted children don't need psychologists." My reply was, "I think they do." He later recommended that I work with Professor Gary Davis because of his interest in creativity. Probably because of Buck's early under-achievement and remarkable creativity, the topic aligned perfectly with my area of interest. I remained in school psychology, but my disser-tation research ultimately focused on gifted creativity. I developed a creativity instrument—GIFT)—which is still used to identify highly creative children who may not necessarily be high achievers. It was based on children's creative interests and independence. My research was based on the biographies of creatively gifted adults—many of whom were not high achievers in childhood. Instead, they questioned the status quo and had many interests. They were curious and imaginative. They like to take things apart to see how they worked. They were independent and persevering. I developed the creativity instrument (GIFT) as part of my doctoral dissertation.

Although I never took a course in gifted education and completed my internship as a regular school psychologist at Webster School in Watertown, I remained determined to specialize in working with gifted children.

You may wonder how my original goal of earning a master's degree eventually evolved into pursuing a Ph.D. As I neared completion of my master's under the guidance of Professor Giebink, he pointed out that I was only six credits and a doctoral dissertation away from a Ph.D.—and he strongly encouraged me to continue. Although I felt inadequate compared to other younger graduate students, he emphasized that my extensive experience with students—especially our own children—would be a significant asset in my work. He even waived the entrance exam, assuring me that my nearly all-A average gave him full confidence in my ability to succeed as a doctoral candidate. I am so appreciative to Professor Giebink for his encouragement, and I don't think I ever found the opportunity to thank him.

It took me eight years to complete my graduate education for my PhD. I received my degree at the same graduation ceremony as our daughter, Ilonna, received her bachelor's degree. She graduated at age 18 and I at age 40. She was so young because she was so unchallenged in high school that she began taking two courses at UW Madison when she was a junior in high school at age 14. She earned As in her college classes, took computer science with 500 students and earned the highest score in the class. Those experiences made it clear that she belonged in college early.

My Careers After Graduate School

After completing my training and earning my school psychologist license, I discovered there was no established career path for someone specializing in gifted children. Not only that, Eric and Sara were still at home, and I wasn't confident that I could work full time yet. Instead, I found an unusual opportunity to teach basic psychology in a small Catholic college—Mount Mary College in Milwaukee. I had so little confidence in myself, and I was terrified about teaching. The environment of teaching with mostly nuns was one of total support. Sister Helen Frances was Chair of the department and she and other nuns were very encouraging and helpful. Classes were small, under 30 students, so I bravely began teaching and absolutely loved it. Furthermore, my students really enjoyed me, and I always received excellent student evaluations.

After my two years of part-time work, they offered me a full-time position. I expanded my teaching load to include Development Psychology and Tests and Measurements, and during the summers, I taught professional development courses for teachers on Gifted Education and Teaching Creatively in the Classroom.

By that time, gifted education was becoming increasingly in demand. My major professor, Gary Davis, was invited to author a textbook for preparing teachers of the gifted—even though he actually knew very little about the subject. I felt honored when he invited me to join him in writing the first edition of Education of the Gifted and Talented. That book is now in its seventh edition. Gary served as the lead author for the first five editions. When he became ill, I stepped into the lead role and invited Del Siegle, a professor at the University of Connecticut, to join me for the 6th and 7th editions. It has been the leading textbook in gifted education for many years. Although I've taught courses in gifted education at Mount Mary College and in many professional development settings, neither Gary nor I had ever actually taken a course in the subject.

Family Achievement Clinic

As I continued to teach psychology at Mount Mary, a strange situation began to cause stress. I unintentionally inspired many of my students to major in psychology, but Mount Mary did not have or want to have psychology as a potential major. Students could only major in a combination of psychology and sociology (Behavioral Sciences). Also, although I continued to love teaching, I really wanted to do clinical counseling and specialize in gifted students. I could only do clinical work with supervision. Dr. Frances Culbertson, a professor at University of Wisconsin-Whitewater who also had an interest in gifted education, kindly offered to supervise me in a part-time private practice. I, thus, opened a small office in Milwaukee and specialized in gifted children. I named it Family Achievement Clinic. My clinic became very busy, and I soon recognized I couldn't manage both the clinical work and my teaching responsibilities. So, with some hesitation, I resigned from my position at Mount Mary and joined Directions Counseling Center at Watertown Hospital, where I also established a second location of the Family Achievement Clinic. That also soon became very, very popular and I needed help and more independence.

I transitioned out of the hospital setting and into private office spaces in Watertown, Oconomowoc, and Milwaukee. I hired Michael Cornale as Assistant Director, and over time, expanded the practice to include 16 other counselors and psychologists in four offices, including one in Madison. We had become an exciting professional business helping many families with gifted children.

We also began summer institutes for training teachers at Olympia in Oconomowoc. Hundreds of teachers arrived for a week of intense gifted training, and we continued these workshops for ten years. I'll describe these further in the next chapter.

I'm skipping some important chapters here, but we'll come back to them. With Buck's help, I had established an educational research organization, begun writing my own books, and was invited to speak at schools—addressing parents and educators about my Trifocal Model for Achievement. These three activities happened simultaneously as I became better known. I'll write about each for clarity in three separate sections.

Educational Assessment Service, Inc.

Placing my experiences on a clear timeline is difficult, but I became interested in educational research early in my graduate studies. Although I found statistics to be a challenging subject, I quickly recognized its value in identifying what truly supports effective student learning. I loved my research projects despite my lack of confidence as a student. I remember designing a test for Eric's preschool class to evaluate how much knowledge they had before kindergarten. The purpose was a project in test construction. Then five years later, I used the same test for Sara's preschool class, compared scores and discovered they performed much better than Eric's had done. My paper hypothesized that the educational television program, Sesame Street—which nearly all the children in Sara's class watched—had a significant educational impact on her preschool peer group.

Around the same time, our friend Babs Bortin, who worked as an evaluator for school programs in Milwaukee, shared some of her work with me. As I reviewed it, I began to think that perhaps I could do something similar for schools as well. I might even get some statistical assistance from my statistician husband. So, Buck and I decided to form a corporation called Educational Assessment Service, Inc. (EASI). Maybe we could make it "easi" to do some difficult school evaluations.

I have no idea how I managed to get school evaluation contracts with St. Paul and Minneapolis schools, but I did. I was soon flying back and forth searching out their test data, analyzing it and writing reports for their school boards.

We converted our former pig house into a cozy office space, even thinking that if the business didn't work out, we could use it as a guest house. I hired assistants and the business worked out very well. Our world soon expanded beyond educational assessment for schools to include Apple Publishing, which published my books and assessment tools— Underachievement Syndrome: Causes and Cures, Group Inventory for Finding Creative Talent (GIFT), Group Inventory for Finding Interests (GIFFI), and the Preschool and Kindergarten Interest DEscriptor (PRIDE). At times, we had as many as ten employees working in our small office, and we even added a large shed to store all our newsletters and publications. Each school presentation would bring more requests for newsletters and books, and I added considerably more books, as well. The initial book "Underachievement Syndrome: Causes and Cures" will be explained below.

As I mentioned earlier, the most successful enterprise by Educational Assessment Service Inc. was a summer workshop for teachers of gifted students. Each summer, we attracted 300 to 500 teachers to Olympia in Oconomowoc, where we guided them in strategies to reverse underachievement in gifted students. Mike Cornale and several staff member from the Family Achievement Clinic helped lead the workshops, which were both practical and inspiring. We even added a touch of fun with entertainment at Apple Bapple Orchard, including a tractor-wagon ride through the trees. Teachers attended from across the country, and Mount Mary College sponsored continuing education credits The workshops were not only highly successful—they were energizing and memorable for everyone involved.

CHAPTER 10

The Books I've Written and My Radio Show

I learned a lot by writing books while working with Professor Gary A. Davis on our textbook. Engaging writing meant blending solid research with plenty of real life examples from home and school—and even a bit of humor between the lines and pages.

The model we applied in our clinical work proved successful in helping many students overcome underachievement. That's what brought parents into our clinic. Changes had to be made for the students, the parents, and the teachers. Overempowerment often occurred with gifted children, and their internalized pressures of competition felt very real to them—even when those pressures were unintentionally created by loving, well-meaning families and educators. For example, overpraise caused perfectionistic pressures. Teaching students to develop a work ethic and resilience was absolutely necessary. Carol Dweck's theories were part of my thinking before her work became well known. I knew I wanted to write a book about reversing under-achievement but didn't have the confidence to believe any publisher would be interested in it.

Jim Webb, Ph.D., a well-known professor and educational publisher and owner of Great Potential Press (when it was small) was also a small plane pilot. Who could imagine that he would land at the Watertown Airport with airplane problems and decide to contact me and visit our farm? I knew him from the National Association for Gifted Children (NAGC) conferences. He came for only a few hours while his small plane was being repaired—just enough time for me to share my idea for a book about underachievement. I bravely asked him "Jim, would you consider publishing my book if I wrote one?" "Great idea," Jim said. "I could do that, or if you'd like, I could even tell you how to publish it yourself." He was soon gone to fly away home, but I was really excited!

Wow, that was a lot to think about! It was enough inspiration to start me writing. I titled the book "Underachievement Syndrome: Causes and Cures," and Gary Davis was kind enough to read it through, offer editorial suggestions, and encouraged me throughout the process.

When I was all done, Buck said, "maybe your book will become a best seller. We should publish it ourselves. I can even put a family photo on the cover." So, we decided to do that, and when the self-published book was ready, Jim and other publishers were happy to sell it for us. Parents and teachers really liked it. I decided to send a copy to my favorite Wisconsin public radio program announcer, Tom Clark.

Tom surprisingly arranged to interview me at 6:30 a.m. for a total of five minutes. I was excited and nervous. No sooner did I hang up the phone when he called me back and told me I had described him when he was a little boy. He said he was an underachiever with "pencil anxiety." He asked me to come on the show and answer parent call-in questions. Little did I know at that time that I would hear the same comments from almost every other male radio announcer afterwards. So, I drove to Madison every two weeks and answered parents' questions about their children on public radio. I became really well-known in Wisconsin.

My clinic clients increased, and my books sold really well. Then I followed up with another book, "How to Parent So Children Will Learn," also self-published at first. When Wisconsin Public Radio held their fundraisers, they often invited me to speak—and during my segments the station consistently received a strong response in listener contributions. They would always raise the most money in my hour. Tom Clark was a very good co-host. Of course, I did all this as a volunteer.

The more people heard me, the more my books sold. My speaking opportunities and clinic clients multiplied. For my early talks I offered my services free of charge. That changed as schools happily paid me first hundreds, then thousands of dollars to talk to parents and teachers. My work was really helping gifted underachievers to correct their underachieving patterns. Then Tom Clark suggested that it was time to take our talk show to public radio nationally.

So, Family Talk with Sylvia Rimm became a national program featured on approximately 35 public radio stations. Needless to say, I enjoyed doing the programs, but much more was to happen, surprisingly in the future.

My Syndicated Columns

I figured that if I could write books and answer parent questions during talks and radio interviews, then surely I could also respond to those parents who preferred the privacy of asking their questions in written form. In those years, everyone read local newspapers, and question/answer syndications were common. I thought perhaps I could at least try that for our local community in Watertown where I was already well known for my School Board participation. The Watertown Daily Times was happy to give me a try, so I began my Sylvia Rimm, On Raising Kids column. After a few months of being published locally, we began distributing my columns to other communities—particularly those in the Madison and Milwaukee areas. My charge was minimal, and I soon had 15 newspaper subscriptions. It was time to try syndication, and I received an immediate response from plenty of newspapers, including Milwaukee and Cleveland, that joined my readership. Yes, that added to my school talks and workshops and to my book prominence. Educational Assessment Service, Inc. was busier than ever!

Chapter 11

Our Key Largo Days

Winters in Wisconsin were long and very cold. We were working hard and raising four kids, and it never occurred to us to get away for actual vacations in winter. Conferences for both me and Buck did take us places for short working vacations, and we visited family members in summer, but it wasn't until Sara was a teenager that we finally decided to take a winter trip to Florida. David and his medical school friends were in Key Largo, exploring the then-new sport of windsurfing. He suggested that we rent a cottage nearby for a few days—so we did. We immediately fell in love with Key Largo, and Buck and David also fell in love with windsurfing.

The magnificent sunsets, stunning blue waters, and comfortable temperatures were irresistible—and of course, we quickly found a realtor who was more than happy to show us around. We easily discovered a three-bedroom home on the bay, on the cheaper side of the Keys, and bought it quick as a wink. It lacked the proper sunset view, but it had the potential for a top of the house porch that would provide that. David's windsurfing friends worked with him to build a small sunset deck that provided an incredible view, and we were all set.

We loved it, and it wasn't long before we began planning family vacations for Thanksgiving week, Christmas break, and several weeks in late January and February. This was all before the grandchildren were born. It worked well because it even included many, if not all, of the children's and eventually grandchildren's birthdays.

Our first house was relatively small, and Miriam was the only grand-baby that visited it. I do remember me riding with her on the seat on the back of my bike, singing "A, you're Adorable, B, you're Beautiful, C, you're a Cutie full of Charm." I'm not sure if that taught her the alphabet. It's likely she had already learned it at home, but she sang along with me. We had plenty of windsurfer boards, canoes and even a small boat to take us out on beautiful Florida Bay. The Fish House and Snappers had already lured us to restaurant eating. Plenty of yellowtail and Florida lobster and fish dips were part of the fun. Cycling was also great in the Keys, so we began quite a bike collection. Everyone loved the Keys so, of course, I contacted our realtor again who found us a larger home with about five bedrooms on North Bounty Lane with a great deck where we could watch sunsets together without any need for construction.

Eight more grandchildren followed, and soon the bedrooms were full, sleeping bags piled up, and bicycles, boards, and boats seemed to multiply. Our happy grandchildren founded the Coconut and Coral Store. where they sold shells, homemade shell jewelry, and other treasures—always at bargain penny prices. I don't think they sold much except to family, but they certainly enjoyed their business establishment.

All the kids swam, snorkeled and windsurfed—and they also put on plays and musicals to entertain the adults during every holiday. And yes, there was plenty of fishing, grilling, baking, and eating—chocolate chip cookies made by Sara, or special ones without chocolate chips just for Popity.

Sunsets were magnificent and we would even get to see an occasional green flash. Kids slept in beds, sofas and in sleeping bags on the floor. We were crowded, so we again needed to move to an even bigger and better place on South Bounty Lane. Each time we sold we made some profit so that encouraged our spreading out. I remember many joyful New Year 's parties with Miriam, Ben and Avi on the top deck of the new house, and dozens of Thanksgiving productions performed by Rachel, Hannah, Dan, Isaac, Sam and Davida.

Our 50th Golden Anniversary party brought dozens of family members together for a joyful celebration in the Keys, and many came to visit on separate occasions as well. By that time, we had a couple of boats—one for ocean fishing for the boys and one for dragging kids on rafts around the bay. We did so much boating and exploring, and we even boated down to Key West a couple of times.

In the spirit of land purchase, we would buy adjoining lots each time we bought a house. The lots protected our privacy when we lived there and provided some financial gains when we sold them later. Property prices in Key Largo continued to increase as more people discovered this vacation paradise.

CHAPTER 12

The Cleveland, Ohio Move

We were so happy in Wisconsin and never really thought we would move again. Our children were all out of high school and mostly out of college and into graduate school or careers. We were traveling a great bit and almost totally contented. Then Buck received an invitation to apply for a chairmanship of a department at Case Western Reserve University Medical School in Ohio. Yikes, he just couldn't resist going for an interview and, of course, they loved him. They wanted him to chair the Department of Epidemiology and Biostatistics. What a dilemma. How could I give up all my successful enterprises housed in Wisconsin?

We thought about it and discussed possible optional positions for me at Case as well. That made it equally exciting. We chose Metro Health Medical Center, where I could serve as a clinical professor, teach medical students, and establish a new Family Achievement Clinic within the Departments of Psychiatry and Pediatrics.

Cleveland Public Radio was already carrying my radio show from the Wisconsin broadcasts and agreed to continue airing it—while also producing the national version. However, I would have to host it on my own this time, without Tom Clark.

I was giving up a lot in Wisconsin, and we were both tentatively leaving our beautiful home on the farm. We were determined to come back to Wisconsin every summer, so we were planning to continue EASI at the farm. It was too big to move. It did become the end of our Apple Bapple Orchard. (Considering it was losing money, that was a reasonably good change.) Also, I had to sell my clinics in Wisconsin for a next to nothing price to my colleagues because I knew that would be only fair. They had helped me build it, and they continued clinics in Watertown, Milwaukee and Madison for quite a long time thereafter.

We did sell the building used for our Oconomowoc clinic.

Moving was not an easy decision, but we finally decided it was time to take the new challenge. By the time we moved to Cleveland, and I accepted the position at Metro Health Medical Center, I had already established a national reputation as a specialist in gifted children. It was likely not the best hospital to work at because it was an urban hospital, but I developed a group there and helped train interns. Although it wasn't the ideal setting, families from across the Cleveland area recognized that I could help their gifted children succeed—and my ongoing radio program played a key role in attracting them.

I consulted with teachers, gave professional education lectures and saw many families. Then something else happened that was unique. To explain I must review more of my history from Wisconsin. As you may recall, my Wisconsin clinic grow quickly after I began giving free talks to parents at schools, focusing specifically on gifted underachievement. Around that time, I was interviewed by Tom Clark on Wisconsin Public Radio at 6:30 a.m. for a five-minutes segment—shortly after I had published my first book, Underachievement Syndrome: Causes and Cures. As you likely recall, that brought me to my national public radio program.

Before I explain more about my exciting growing career, let me share about our new homes in Cleveland.

Our Beautiful Home on Lake Erie

After leaving our beautiful home on the farm in Wisconsin, almost any place would have felt like a disappointment—and there was certainly no hope of finding a similar farm near Cleveland. Although Buck's work was on the east side of Cleveland, we had already heard about the east side being the "snow belt." We briefly searched for homes in the area, but they were crowded and expensive. And the more we heard about the "snow belt," the more memories of Buffalo and Wisconsin winters convinced us to head west instead. Living on the lake seemed tempting and lake homes near Cleveland were expensive. Finally, we decided to rent an apartment for starters so we would have more time to explore.

It took two lakeside rentals before we found the perfect home with amazing views and only two serious problems. It was over 100 years old and needed much remodeling, and it was a long commute to our offices. The beautiful sunset view was impossible to deny ourselves, and the home was plenty roomy for family visits. Furthermore, we could do the major remodeling before we moved in while still living in our rental house a mile away. Anyway, we have no regrets about that beautiful home and still live there now more than 30 years later. Every first-time visitor announces "WOW!" when they enter and see the beautiful lake view through our living room windows!

Boating on Lake Erie and Wisconsin Summers

With no apple orchard to keep Buck busy, his love of boating — rooted in childhood and rekindled in Key Largo— made spending time on the beautiful waters of Lake Erie an absolute priority. We started with a small boat but that was "much too dangerous for such a large lake." Small boat #1 got traded for a larger boat and a still larger boat. Spring, summer and fall fun included boating to the islands and even to Canada. With our bikes on the boat, we could explore the islands and the Canadian small towns, and we truly did have terrific fun experiences. Our friends could even join us on our boat to watch fireworks on the 4th of July.

Then somehow, the boats got "too big"—both in size and for Buck to navigate, as well as ridiculously expensive to fill with gas. We decided we had outgrown boating. We sold our boats and instead searched out places on the "small boat" lakes in Wisconsin. We could get back to visiting the farm, as well. Buck really missed the farm.

Thus, we found some places on Nagawicka and Pewaukee where we combined lake and farm fun and even had some time to spend with our Wisconsin friends.

Chapter 13

NBC's Today Show

Now, I'll get back to describing my career "miracles."

A high school friend of Ilonna's, Happy Luchsinger, was a producer for the Today Show. She was pregnant for the first time, and she came back to visit family in Wisconsin and just happened to hear my call-in show on public radio. She then convinced NBC's Today Show to try some parenting segments with me on their national morning Today Show. In 1992, when this took place, there was little or no internet and television was almost all powerful. Morning news was mandatory listening and NBC's Today Show was ranked #1 in that very competitive market. Since we didn't even have a television set in our home, I knew very little— if anything—about it when Happy contacted me. So I wasn't particularly enthusiastic about going to New York. She asked me to do three short five-minute segments in February. It just so happened that there was an absolute blizzard on the entire east coast the day of my first segment. It was so bad that all the New York airports and most schools on the east coast were closed. I had to fly to Boston and take a train to New York to get there. I remember the day with snow piled high and drifted everywhere and almost no automobile traffic. My first topic was on gifted children who underachieve—the same topic as my first book. Happy had prepared me well. She explained that I had to give a post office box and an 800 number (no internet in those days), and I had to offer to send some information on the topic. While we were in Wisconsin, I had published a regular newsletter on parenting topics. So, of course, I had written an issue of the newsletter on gifted underachievement.

I was mighty nervous sitting in the Green Room—but even more so during the interview, as I explained how very capable students can become defensive and begin avoiding their work. I specifically talked about boy problems with "pencil anxiety" and girl problems with perfectionism.

After my first five-minute segment on TV, I received 20,000 phone calls and 5,000 letters requesting newsletters, and, as a result, I also received a contract from NBC to become a regular contributing correspondent to NBC's Today Show. Thereafter, for eight years I flew to New York once a month and did five-minute segments on parenting. When I walked into the Green Room, people waiting to be on the show would often ask me parenting questions. I was a bit of a local consultant. NBC gave me a contract and paid me $1,000 each time I came to New York, as well as the cost of my flight and a beautiful hotel room at the very fancy Essex House. I guess you might say I "hobnobbed" with the "stars." Katie Couric was the leading host at that time. She had two children and most of the regular contributors and producers had young children, as well. Anne Curry, Matt Lauer and Bryant Gumbel also had children, as did other invited guests. There was much interest from the audience and that's what really counted.

Little did I realize at that time how important Happy was in my career. I found out later that our children's reputations were critical to my being invited to the show. I think they'd handsome earlier guest psychologists who were a bit too permissive with their views on children behavior and drug use, and Katie wanted reassurance that our children were good students and responsible citizens. All the stars wanted very personal advice. Although I wasn't very "classy," I gave good common-sense advice. Here is the quotation that Katie later gave me for my website:

> *"Dr. Rimm is a welcome voice of calm and reason—someone who offers practical advice, with almost immediate results. She's a guardian angel for families who need a little or a lot of guidance."*

As for Katie Couric, I greatly admired her. I did want her to be part of my best-selling book, "See Jane Win,", but she was very cautious. She explained kindly to me why she couldn't chance participating because so much was taken out of context when one is a TV star. I was thrilled to assist with child advice for the stars, so I didn't even consider asking other Today Show stars to be part of my book. I did manage to attract a few NBC weather people and behind-the-scenes participants.

People in Cleveland knew me mainly from my radio program. Even New Yorkers would stop me on the street during those years and recognize me as being on the Today Show. My public radio show received even more attention once I was a Today Show expert. Families listened to me regularly at home and in their cars on the way to church and many called in parenting questions.

Our children loved my being on the Today Show, too, and they tuned in whenever possible. My mother-in-law, Bess, never missed a program but she argued that they should have given me more time on the show. One time David and his family came to New York and held up a big poster that said, 'Sylvia Rimm Raised My Dad'. All our children came to the show at least once in New York.

The eight years of flying to New York, waiting in the star-filled NBC Green Room, and being interviewed by Katie Couric, Bryant Gumbel, Ann Curry, Matt Lauer, and many others felt like a dream—moments of unexpected fame.

I was prepared for every show by a TV producer. Happy was my first producer, but she only produced a few of my programs. Then she left the show to have her baby and care for her. She also introduced me to Pierre Lehu, who became my agent and found many other speaking and media opportunities for me. Then Janet Schiller took over production and worked with me the rest of my time on the show. She would prepare my host for each program so they were ready to question me. Janet, too, was great to work with.

Ann Curry and Matt Lauer were delightful and easy to work with for my segments. There were no surprises, but both made me feel confident and appreciated. Bryant Gumbel only interviewed me a few times, but he caused me the most anxiety. He was a very nice guy, but he was definitely the most independent and didn't always go with the program. I could expect the unexpected, so I had to be quick thinking and ever ready for surprises. There were other hosts whose names I've forgotten, but I soon built self-confidence, and the Today Show seemed to have confidence in me.

Books by the Dozens

Many viewers bought my books. Before long, major publishers took interest in my work. Underachievement Syndrome was revised slightly and re-released as *Why Bright Kids Get Poor Grades and What You Can Do About It*. That was soon followed by additional titles, including *How to Parent So Children Can Learn, Keys to Parenting the Gifted Child, Raising Preschoolers* (written at the special request of Katie Couric) and many more.

Why Bright Kids Get Poor Grades and What You Can Do About It sold over 75,000 additional copies. As a self-published paperback, it had also already sold 75,000 books.

My Best-Selling Book and the Oprah Winfrey Show

While working at Metro Health Medical Center and writing books, I saw an opportunity to create a special book focused on girls and women—one that would celebrate the expanding roles and opportunities available to women. I was a member of what was then known as "The Silent Generation." We had gone through World War II and were glad to be at peace. Women were mostly hoping to be mothers and homemakers. My personal teachers had been mainly unmarried women. Only a few women, after their children were in school, dared to enter high level professions. That was changing quickly, and a new generation of women were entering all careers including those where women hadn't dared to tread. I wanted to investigate whether women could be successful and happy in careers and manage a good family life. Our daughters were members of this new generation. I was still on the Today Show and I was hoping they would give me the opportunity to present my important research in my new book.

Metro Health supported the idea, and I had staff to help gather and organize the research—as well as daughters and daughters-in-law who assist with conducting interviews. It was an ideal opportunity. I selected 12 career fields—four traditional to women and eight that had earlier been closed to women. We searched all over the country for women who wished to participate. With help from radio, TV, and family members, I recruited women in these 12 different career fields—women who saw themselves as fulfilled both in their professional lives and in their roles within their families. They were given application forms to qualify for those characteristics. Data collection took at least a year.

When the project was complete, it became clear that the most important key to lasting success was resilience in the face of competition. Our daughter-in-law, Janet, came up with the perfect name for the book: *See Jane Win!*

See Jane Win became an interview on The Today Show and soon began selling well. Then I received a call from the Oprah Winfrey Show. They wanted to do a few trial phone interviews with me on other topics, none of which actually went on the show. I was feeling discouraged when I suddenly received a request to do an entire show on See Jane Win. Contributors were also invited, and all guests received copies of the book. Wow—my anxiety went over the top and so did our sale of books. *See Jane Win* went to #1 on the *New York Times* Best Seller List and stayed on top for at least five weeks. It was soon published in paperback and in many countries and the numbers went far beyond 150,000 copies.

The success of the book led to further invitations for keynote addresses and requests for follow-up titles, including *How Jane Won* and *See Jane Win for Girls.* It was very exciting, and even Case Medical School and Metro Health Medical Center were very proud to have me on their faculty and staff.

Cruising the World

My book tours took me all over the country. Public radio featured me weekly for over a dozen years, and my syndicated column, "Sylvia Rimm on Raising Kids"—which began in Watertown, Wisconsin—eventually appeared in more than 50 newspapers across the country. Features in People magazine and other Sunday magazine sections of newspapers made me a familiar voice to young and old alike. Keynote talks across the U.S. and in countries such as England, Spain, France, Saudi Arabia, Australia, New Zealand, Israel, Qatar, Jordan, Italy, Hong Kong and more gave me the opportunity to speak with educators, parents, and grandparents around the globe—even aboard Crystal Cruise Lines as I traveled the seas. I was fortunate to circle the globe on the Queen Mary II with my cousin, Vivian Singer, sharing insights on raising happy achieving children with international audiences.

My experiences cruising the world were so important that I added cruises for my family for adventures. I need to summarize my travels to say that I have been to all 50 states in our country, and many provinces in Canada.

My alphabet of 50 countries from A-Z (if I remove the "New" from New Zealand) is shown below. I've probably forgotten a few. Africa, Algeria, Andes, Argentina, Canada, Caribbean, Chile, Columbia, Cozumel, Denmark, Ecuador, England, France, Galapagos Islands, Germany, Greenland, Holland, Hong Kong, Iceland, Ireland, Israel, Italy, Japan, Jordan, Korea, Latvia, Lithuania, Mexico, Mongolia, Norway, Panama Canal, Poland, Portugal, Puerto Rico, Qatar, Russia, Saudi Arabia, Sicily, Singapore, Spain, Sweden, Syria, Turkey, Uruguay, Vietnam and Zealand (New).

Oh, how fortunate I've been—what thrills I experienced! When Buck got tired of cruising, friends and even granddaughter, Miriam, joined in for the excursions. And when I extended cruise offers to family, grandchildren and even great grandchildren joined us. What a beautiful world! How fortunate I have been!

CHAPTER 14
The World of Hospital Politics

We had some wonderful times and some strange ones. For Buck, as Chair of the Department of Epidemiology and Biostatics, he did a great job, and we also had some lovely parties and international trips. We thought he did an excellent job, but over time, the administration changed, bringing new expectations and changed leadership. Despite that, he continued his work in research and teaching.

For me, things did become very strange. Metro Health Medical Center was on the wrong side of town for attracting parents who were concerned about their gifted children. Few parents who lived nearby were familiar with the term gifted education. Although I had no doubt I could identify many gifted children in the area, I found the parents and teachers often held lower expectations for their children. I remember one family brought a child to me who thought their daughter was gifted but actually only registered a 70 IQ. My radio program on Cleveland Public Radio did attract families, although many would have preferred a different office location or neighborhood. My move to the Today Show aroused great interest at Metro Health. The vice president took me aside and asked me how Metro could better serve my clinic. We were soon moved to the suburbs with very fancy offices, staff and graduate students.

The first five years Metro encouraged my travel and publicized our clinic, and we attracted Dr. Dan Weinberger and Dr. Christine Brewer. Dr. Dan was an excellent staff person, and Dr. Christine came in as a graduate student and became a regular staff member. Dr. Ed Amend, experienced in gifted, joined us for several years, and we were truly on a roll and a known name locally and nationally.

While I was at Metro Health, I did small group teaching of medical students when they went through pediatrics and psychiatry rounds. I really loved that. I believe the students enjoyed the classes on parenting gifted children—especially since many of them were gifted themselves. They often related deeply with the discussions, gaining insight to their own feelings of pressure, perfectionism, and success. I hated giving up the teaching.

Although our clinic remained active, someone in a high-level office at Metro Health decided that Psychology and Counseling departments were not financially sustainable. We were told that all staff needed to increase our hours and cut our budget costs. Finally, I was told we'd have to leave because of our financial losses even despite our radio and TV renown.

Buck and I chatted about that, and he suggested he write a letter bragging about his wife to Cleveland Clinic. Cleveland Clinic was interested and invited us to a suburban office. I was still traveling and speaking all over the world, our clinic was busy, but after about two years, I was again told that Psychology and Counseling "just doesn't bring in enough money." They gave me ample time to explore private clinic options and even sent me home with thousands of newsletters they have printed—many of which we still have today.

CHAPTER 15

Back to FAC

After seven years of working at hospitals, I began to explore beginning my own Family Achievement Clinic private practice again. After meeting with various clinics, it appeared to be complicated. I finally met with Roxanne Miller at Humanistic Counseling Center (HCC). She agreed to incorporate Family Achievement Clinic with HCC and make it cost effective for all of us. So, Dan Weinberger, Christine Brewer, and I held weekly meetings to discuss cases our shared cases, while Roxanne generously allowed us to use clinic offices on both the east and west sides of Cleveland. We've been with Humanistic for 24 years. We continued to use our Wisconsin office for making clinic appointments, arranging talks and selling books. Barb Gregory stayed with our Wisconsin office to orchestrate our small clinic staff.

We have been busy over these years at a pace each of us felt comfortable with. Things slowed to an almost stop with COVID, but virtual meetings by computer got us through those worst clinic years.

CHAPTER 16

Menlo Park Academy

Menlo Park Academy was established as a charter school for gifted students, and after about two years, the school recognized the importance of having dedicated staff to develop programs for the social-emotional needs of gifted children. I was invited to work part-time to help develop the program. At first, I was their only social-emotional staff member. It was only a small school. I soon invited Christine Brewer and Dan Weinberger to join us, and Christine remained with us for most of those years—except during the difficult period when she bravely battled leukemia. As they expanded, they hired full-time staff, and Christine and I continue only part-time.

Working in a school keeps me in touch with the reality of issues that many gifted students experience. I've been working with the school for more than 18 years and hope to continue for several more.

CHAPTER 17

From Key Largo to Naples

After so many wonderful years in Key Largo, a hurricane hit our home. We completed the repairs for our house, but it suddenly felt like we were getting older and the drive to Key Largo from the airport was long. Our children urged us to find something smaller and easier to reach. We were searching the west coast of Florida when our cousins, Larry and Celia Brown, invited us to visit Naples, Florida. We fell in love with what seemed like the most beautiful nature preserve in the world.

As usual, the buying took two tries. First, a small condo at St. Pierre's and then a larger one so I could have office space, and we could have visitors at Dorchester. The beaches and berm are magnificent, and we had no regrets except that COVID stole much time in Florida away from us. And last but not least, Dad's health became worse and sadly now he's gone. Naples is still wonderful, but lonely and it is harder to make friends, but if I stay well, and I hope I will, I do have lots of family visitors to enjoy this beautiful world with me.

CHAPTER 18

Why Do I Keep Working?

I'm far beyond the typical age of retirement, but I do believe I continue to help families. Sometimes it only takes my guiding them to make small changes but that can make large differences. Other times, of course, problems can be very complex, and positive changes are slow in coming. It's those occasional, heartfelt messages from former clients or their parents that remind me I'm still making a difference —and they're what keep me committed to continuing my work in private practice.

Here's a letter I recently wrote to my children on this topic:

> Hi all,
>
> I'm sure you sometimes think your grandmom is meshugah (crazy) because at almost age 90 she's still working. Every once in a while, I receive a reminder. I just received a letter from a family in North Dakota (I think I saw them about 25 years ago). It was a Happy Easter card to thank me for helping their son (now a father) and all the people on the Indian reservation in northern North Dakota. I spoke to them on teaching and parenting gifted children. I remember it only because it was the coldest day I ever experienced in January--very far below 0, and they flew me there on a small private plane. The family also thanked me for helping their Indian tribe. I can't even imagine how they remember me, but these occasional reminders make

me feel so fortunate for choosing even such a small way to makethe world a little better place. I know that you also understand because you, too, are helping our world become a happier, healthier place.

Much love, Mom, Grandmom and Great Grandmom

I feel like I am still making a real contribution to helping families. That's a message we gave to our family and that they have heard at every family Bar or Bat Mitzvah. I usually began by sharing how crucial it was that my parents were able to immigrate to this country, how deeply Judaism shaped our values, and how important learning was in our family. I have truly lived the American Dream, and I wanted our grandchildren to realize that they, too, carry a responsibility—to make their own meaningful contributions toward creating a better world. Buck also gave them another message, and it too was an important one. He said, "Get your doctorate degree in something." That's also an important message as well: when you discover the career path you're passionate about, aim for the highest possible degree. Doing so gives you the best opportunity to lead and make meaningful contributions in your field. For Buck and me, we thought we'd been very, very fortunate to be able to have careers we felt good about and where we made our small contributions.

A key issue that helped us to be successful, I think, was getting on the cutting edge of a new area. No matter what you choose, you have a little better opportunity for leadership if it's a newly developing field. Buck was one of the founding members of the field of epidemiology. That was an important new field, so he had unusual leadership opportunities. The gifted field was also relatively new and that gave me dramatic opportunities. I've been honored with numerous awards in the field of gifted education and have had the privilege of speaking internationally—delivering keynote addresses around the world on the importance of creativity, gifted education, challenge, reversing underachievement, and fostering resilience. There isn't any way that life can be easy, but if you are fortunate enough to have good health, and you persevere, you can make real contributions to the world.

CHAPTER 19

Our Marriage Relationship

Relationships aren't perfect and when you choose to marry someone, that commitment means truly supporting and caring for them—through health and illness, in both good and hard times. You don't have to marry someone who always has the exact same values, but you must be willing to compromise and come between. The importance of communication in a marriage and being able to talk things through is crucial. Respect is crucial. If parents don't respect each other, children won't respect either of them. If both parents can be role models for their children, children will respect both of them and move forward.

My mother gave me that important message of how important family and love would be, and my mother wasn't an educated woman. She had three or four years of education, but her good common sense and her values were really very important. The love message that came from my parents and how fortunate they were to have each other was the message I wanted to pass on.

I'd like to thank my children for being such amazing, hard-working, kind, good kids. I never had to worry about drugs or meanness or not being respectful. They were always caring and loving to us and loving to their children. They did an amazing job of parenting their children and passing on those wonderful values. We just love to do things with them. There aren't many years left ahead. We always try to plan to get all the family together for adventures or to be together as much as we can. We live in many different cities, but we care about each other a lot.

Even though I talk about the importance of family and how much we love them, we also love them to be independent and have their own lives. We won't dictate their lives, and we respect their values and what they want for their children.

CHAPTER 20

Our Grandchildren

We have nine birth grandchildren, and four are married, so that would be 13 grandchildren. We have six great-grandchildren.

I love my grandparenting. Our children were wonderful parents. I love seeing the kids become independent and doing good things. I do think our grandkids all have that message of being helpful to other people and making a difference in their careers. They're creative and achieving. I don't think we have a single underachiever among them. They're good people and that's what's most important.

As I look back on my life, I feel very, very fortunate. I feel deeply thankful— first, for reasonably good health, for having had a husband who was supportive and respectful and who I, in turn, respected, for the value we placed on education, for the messages we passed on to our children—that they should contribute, and be good, honest people, not solely driven by money, but hopefully their positive contributions. We were very fortunate that we were not caught in the Holocaust. We have a commitment to keep our country free, provide religious freedom, and opportunities for immigrants to get an education. We have a world obligation to help people to be what they can be. It's a message I'm very thankful for as I am for my good health. I truly feel I've lived the American Dream, and I sincerely thank all those who have read my book—for your part in shaping my happy, lucky, and wonderful life.

Letter to Cousin Bob's Family After He Passed Away in June 2023

I'm so sorry I couldn't be with you all at Bob's funeral. As you know, I loved Bob very much and we were especially close as children. It was ironic that my husband, Buck, died on Bob's birthday but, unfortunately, he was moving toward death when Bob died (two men I loved).

I hope you can share with family my little piece below because no one who is alive now, but me, knew him as well when he was growing up. Here is what I remember:

> My cousin Bobby was almost like a brother to me. While I don't remember his baby years (or mine for that matter), by school age we spent lots of time together. We both went to #1 School, and he was only one grade behind me. I think Uncle Challie drove him to school because I don't remember walking there with him, but we always walked home for lunch together because Aunt Idy worked in a factory during World War II and she couldn't be home at lunch time. My mommy made lunch for both of us. We walked together, sang together and told each other jokes. One day we had snow flurries and the song for the day (usually sung by Bing Crosby) was "Let It Snow," so Bobby and I were running, skipping and jumping as we dashed into the house for lunch singing, "When the weather outside is frightful and the fire is so delightful, we'll turn the lights

way down low and let it snow, let it snow, let it snow." As we moved our song into the kitchen, my mother who was preparing our delicious lunch, said "why no lettuce?" Can you imagine our giggles?

Bobby and I played baseball together and believe it or not, I could hit the ball better than him and even run faster. My sisters called me a tomboy. But when it came to baseball knowledge, I knew nothing compared to Bobby. He knew every player, every team, every record. I tried to learn them from him, but I just couldn't remember much. At least I could listen to him, admire and ask him questions.

Aunt Idy would ask Bobby why he couldn't get As like Simi and why he couldn't write as well as Simi. Uncle Challie would say "he was a very smart kid" and Simi thought he was too but like many other boys, he didn't like to write.

What he did like to do was build things with sticks and blocks and erector sets. I liked to build with Bobby, too, but I was never as good or as fast as he was. But I could run fast and was actually a little too daring. I probably should have followed Bobby more. One time we climbed up high on a bleacher in Roosevelt Park. As usual, I was faster and far ahead of Bobby. He was klutzy and fearful. When I got to the top, I told Bobby we could jump off because the grass below was soft. He told me not to do it, and he turned around and went back down slowly and carefully. I called him a "fraidy cat" and proceeded to jump. I can still remember the pain and the tears when I landed. I didn't break any bones, and I didn't tell my parents what I did, but I should have listened to my cousin Bobby. Sometimes Uncle Challie would pick us up from school in his pickup truck. Bobby and I would sit next to him in the front seat. Bobby knew all about how the truck worked and I felt so dumb. I was sure I would never be able to drive.

Uncle Challie would also take us to Bradly Beach or a park on the back of the truck. The whole family would sit on orange crates in the open back part, and we would sing songs together as the truck bumped along the highway or a country road (no seat belts in those days).

Uncle Challie used to bicycle race in Poland where he came from so it became his job to teach all the kids to ride bikes. We all learned on full-sized bikes, and I had to learn standing on the pedals because I couldn't reach the seat. I loved biking, but I can remember quite a few "almost" accidents. You can imagine Bobby's embarrassment when it took him a lot longer to learn. I don't remember if he ever learned.

I hate the idea that Bobby's parents kept telling him that Simi did things better, but I probably liked it then. Bobby and I were such good friends—really like loving siblings.

Most fun of all was when Uncle Challie took us to Yankee Stadium to watch the baseball games. Bobby knew everything about every player and gradually he was teaching me more about sports.

Bobby and I both learned Yiddish and studied at Sholem Aleichem Folk Shule #7. But Bobby also studied for his Bar Mitzvah in a special class for boys. The whole family celebrated his Bar Mitzvah at a huge party. After that, the competition stopped. Bobby suddenly became an excellent student and had lots of A's all through high school. We just stopped competing and loved each other. We did lots of things at the YMHA and went to dances on the roof garden. We both joined Young Judaea and went to Camp Tel Yehudah (not at the same time), and I think Bobby went to Israel too. Bobby met the love of his life through Young Judaea and continued to be the really gifted student that, even then, I suspected he always was. We will all miss Bobby. He was a special cousin to me.

Obituary

It remains difficult and so sad for me to believe that my husband of 66 years has passed away. He was much loved by all his family, and I added his obituary and funeral talks with happy remembrances and much love.

Alfred (Buck) Rimm 1934 - 2023

Alfred Aron Rimm, 89, died on June 28, 2023, leaving a remarkable professional and personal legacy. Born in 1934 to Bess and Ben Rimm, Alfred (also known as Buck) grew up in Atlantic City, NJ where he sold newspapers on the boardwalk, played ball in the streets, and quickly learned to take the path less traveled—which became a theme that was evident throughout his life. Alfred went to college at Rutgers University where he majored in Agriculture and met the love of his life, Sylvia Rimm. Upon graduating, he married Sylvia and launched into graduate school in Dairy Science and Genetics with a two-year break to serve in the Air Force as Captain based in Korea after the Korean War. These years were full of life with two new children 13 months apart and doctoral studies leading to a Ph.D. in Dairy Science and Genetics. Alfred and his family moved 13 times before Alfred found a job in Biostatistics at the Medical College of Wisconsin. Here, he developed a career in epidemiology and biostatistics. His work was innovative yet non-traditional and he pursued ideas related to graft-versus-host disease and racial disparities in Medicare access. In the 1970's, Alfred was very involved in data collection for the new therapy of Bone Marrow Transplantation. He used his statistical skills to participate in the creation of the Center for International Blood & Marrow Transplant Research, which is a Milwaukee-based organization that is celebrating their 50th anniversary this year. He pioneered ideas related to novel methods in the assessment of obesity, including risk factors that lead to diabetes and heart disease. In 1993, Alfred took a new position as Chairman of the Department of Epidemiology and Biostatistics at Case Western Reserve University. This role enabled him to continue his research while also leading a talented group of faculty to address contemporary issues in public health. A few themes stood out during his almost 60-year career—Alfred Rimm was intensely curious and loved to read scientific journals, he thought about ideas a bit differently than others, and he absolutely loved numbers and data. He routinely would ask people to guess the number of heart beats the average person had in a lifetime.

Alfred's personal legacy is colorful and interesting. Together with Sylvia, they had four children, nine grandchildren, and five great grandchildren. Alfred conveyed the importance of education to his family at every opportunity. Like many other dads, Alfred played golf and tennis with his sons. But golf and tennis were not enough—he tended to prefer more unusual activities. When the family moved to Wisconsin, he and his family planted 10,000 fir evergreen trees on two farms in Wisconsin. A few years later, he led his family from his small hobby of planting a few apple trees to a full-fledged apple orchard. Together, the family planted 10,000 apple trees, leading to the creation of Apple Bapple Orchard. Alfred had a lot of creative ideas—some brilliant and some at odds with the forces of gravity. He built a pond for his kids where they could swim in the summer and ice skate in the winter—activities that his kids carried into their adult lives. Each year, he created a path through the 100-acre woods so his family could wander and play in a beautiful natural space, which instilled in his family a tremendous appreciation for the natural world. But, he also thought that a silo would be a workable solution to a water storage problem leading to an effective trickle irrigation system for the apple orchard. Alas, the silo did not hold water. His family fondly remembers Alfred sailboarding into his 70's, saluting when driving past a John Deere store, enjoying intense fishing trips some with many fish, some that were just "boat rides", baling hay with his boys, collecting hobbies (e.g., tropical fish, scuba diving, large-format photography), taking a two-fisted approach to dessert eating, and saying, "none of your business" when asked by a family member at a restaurant, "what will you be ordering from the menu?"

Alfred Rimm will be remembered as a joyfully idiosyncratic person with very creative ideas. Unlike many men in his era, Alfred was tremendously supportive of his wife's career. He was a terrific mentor to everyone who asked for his support. His actions were principled and showed integrity despite the challenges that were thrown his way.

Alfred is survived by his loving wife, Sylvia Rimm, and his four children and their spouses, Ilonna and Joe, David and Janet, Eric and Allison, and Sara and Larry, his nine grandchildren and their spouses, Miriam and Ben, Ben and Shoshana, Avi, Dan and Jess, Rachel, Hannah and Kate, Isaac, Sam and Davida, and his five great grandchildren, Yoni, Zelly, Danny, Elizabeth, and Jacob. He is predeceased by his parents, Bess and Benjamin Rimm, his brother and sisters-in-law, Sigmund Rimm, Carol Rimm, and Barbara Rimm, and his son-in-law, Alan Rimm-Kaufman.

His departure leaves quite a void. We can honor his memory in both serious and humorous ways. Alfred's family encourages others to read and learn, ask important questions about the world, enjoy the companionship of family, plant trees, and even to eat some of his favorite candy, such as black licorice, peanut M&Ms, and Dots (but avoid the red ones).

Message from Ilonna

I am Ilonna Rimm, the oldest daughter, and I'm grateful for the opportunity to speak to you today, although the time is so sad. First of all, I am the black sheep of the Rimm siblings—I have no professor title after my name. In spite of this deficit, my dad did love me so much.

To honor my dad and remind us all of the incredible role of fathers in the lives of their children, I'd like to tell you some stories about how Dad took care of me when I was a little girl, now more than 60 years ago.

My first memories of my dad are from when I was about two or three years old. Dad came home from work, and David my younger brother, and I would sit on his feet as he walked and here is the story of how it happened. When Dad arrived home from work, he said, "Do you want to sit on my feet?" We ran to him and said, "Yay!" We each sat on one foot, and then he would walk, and swinging us into the air as he walked, and we laughed with delight. When he moved his foot up, we went flying up into the air, and it was little scary. But Daddy was taking care of us so we knew that we were safe. In a quiet moment, I can still reexperience the joy of that exciting trip where we traveled at least six or eight inches into the air. What a wonderful memory!

When David and I were a little older, maybe three or four years old, our dad told us his own imaginary fairy tale story about the great white bird. Dad talked about the great white bird that was so large that it could carry children on its back for a ride. David and I listened to every word, spellbound. And Dad described that the great white bird would land, and then two children climbed onto the back of the great white bird for a ride. Those two children were named Sidesbottom and Griselda, which meant that they were a boy and a girl, just like David and me.

When the story came to this point, David and I look happily at each other, thinking that we were like Sidesbottom and Griselda. Then Dad described, in a hushed voice, that the great white bird would take off, and Sidesbottom and Griselda would hold on tight, and go flying into the air. And then, off in the distance, they could see a city where everything was made of gold. And soon, the great white bird landed near the city, and Sidesbottom and Griselda hopped off the bird, and went to explore the city of gold, where all the buildings were gold. It was so exciting, and David and I could hardly believe that we could hear about the incredible flight of the great white bird. In a quiet moment, I can still remember the feeling of wonder from that moment.

Message from David

As the second child of Alfred and Sylvia Rimm, I was born when Alfred was 25 years old. Dad was an incredible father and a huge influence for my career and my life. As we all know, Dad was a numbers guy (and so am I), so I will list the 100 most impactful themes. (Okay, that would take too long; I'll stick to five):

Planting Trees: Thousands of them, initially haphazardly planting hundreds of small seedling pine trees (12" to 15" long), pulling them from buckets of cold water to be sure the roots didn't dry, and placing them in the gap between the shovel held by Dad and the dirt. When I complained that my hands were freezing, Dad instructed me to warm them on the engine block of the tractor so we could finish the job. This was a lesson in persistence for a ten-year-old.

Down the Mississippi River: When I was ten, Dad decided that he wanted to do something special and memorable with his son. In the times before cell phones and GPS, we trailered the boat to Alton, Illinois, where we put it in and, using only charts and visual navigation, spent seven days cruising down the Mississippi ending in Gulfport, Louisiana. Some aspects of the trip did not go according to plan, but there were many amazing memories, and all ended safe and sound back in Wisconsin about two weeks later. This was a lesson in adventure.

Baling Hay: As a teenager, Dad and I were partners in harvesting alfalfa hay in the summer to sell to local farmers for their cattle in the winter. We split the cutting and the raking, but for baling Dad drove the tractor and I piled the 50-pound bales on the wagon, as many as possible before unloading in the barn. After three or four wagon loads, we were both hot and tired. I may have had a beer or two in recovery even though I was not yet 18. This was a lesson in both hard physical work and flexibility.

Medical School: Dad told me I could do anything I wanted to do in life…after I got my MD. As the second child, and in the shadow of Ilonna who had already begun her MD-PhD when I started college,

I thought I would study to go to law school. Though I liked debate and philosophy, ultimately the science courses "picked me." My fascination with chemistry and genetics ultimately led me to pursue an MD-PhD. Now, 34 years since graduation, I can say that I have had a very fulfilling career. He taught me to be aware of those whose main goal is self-aggrandizement and reminded me that the privilege of academia is that the patient is your only shareholder. This was a lesson in wisdom.

Fishing: Dad loved to fish and started me fishing for bluegills through the ice of Lake Nashotah at age six. By the time I was ten or twelve, we would fish for Coho Salmon in Lake Michigan in the boat called, "Mommyhasacrookednose" and even took Eric with us as soon as he was old enough. Later, we began fishing off the reef near Key Largo where we had some epic trips called "schoolies" that included Eric, Alan and other guests and, as soon as they turned 13, Dad's grandchildren. These trips sometime yielded over 50 fish (Dorado and Mahi), while other Keys trips especially in the fall, were "boat rides," meaning no fish at all. This was a lesson in fun, fishing tricks and sometimes patience.

In summary, I was extremely fortunate to be raised by a thoughtful, persistent, adventurous, wise and loving father. He will be in my fondest memories forever.

Message from Eric

Dad's funny sayings—I have given hundreds of talks, but I never write them down until today. As my dad would say, "My memory is shot" so I wrote this down.

My talk is some of my dad's funny sayings only because of all the family, I have the lowest threshold for crying, and if I told anything too serious, we would all be here for 30 minutes while I try to compose myself. Don't worry, I will still cry through the jokes, but I want you all to laugh with me because that will give me a little time.

None of these jokes are to make fun of Dad, but to laugh with him, because that is what he would want. This will be brief!

Some jokes were personal and just for me and some were for the whole family. For example, when I called and Dad answered the phone, I would say, "Hey Dad, this is your good-looking son," to which he, of course, would respond "Hello David."

The next one is a classic one that all the grandkids knew. It was his own personal call to dinner when we were all in Wisconsin, Cleveland or Florida and it was time to go out to a restaurant. "Sim, I'll be in the car." My father was professionally diagnosed with *shpilkes* and always wanted to get going and be on time for our reservation. Mom and Dad were so generous to all of us through the last 50 years!

On the darker side…whenever one of us went on a trip with friends as a young adult, he would send us on our way by saying, "Don't come back in a pine box, it would upset your mother." Dark, but we got the point—it was his way of saying, "I love you."

Dad taught me the classic sports like baseball, football, tennis, golf and even bowling, and got me hooked on the Packers and the Brewers. He was definitely not cheap, but he loved buying those seats in the upper deck to the Brewers game, and then slowly walking down, so by the 8th inning we were sitting 20 rows from the field.

Dad also taught me some less conventional sports like ping pong and billiards. One phrase that still rings true in my nightmares, and David's too I am sure, is from playing pool in the basement. When he hit the final winning shot, he would exclaim with great gusto "Rack-em." The unspoken translation was "I just kicked your ass, rack the balls, we are playing another game." Dad taught us racquetball, too, and always started out every discussion with, "you can win if you use—STRATEGY." His saying here was, "hit it where they ain't, hit the ceiling shot and hit it to their backhand." None of us in the family were great athletes, but we won a few tournaments thanks to Dad's "strategy."

Last but not least, Dad gave me a little bug I still haven't been able to shake.

In fact, some could say I have this like the Alfred Rimm Flu! When I was a kid whenever we would go to the airport to pick up my Grandmom and Pop Pop, who were coming to visit, we would go early to play pinball. He didn't have to give me any funny sayings there to make me laugh and smile. I always prayed my grandparents would come in three hours late on the plane! That was just pure fun, and 50 years later, Allison, Isaac, Hannah and I have built a shrine in our basement complete with ping pong and a full pinball arcade. I am still loving and remembering that experience from 50 years ago. Thanks, Dad, for the fun.

Message from Sara

My dad cared deeply about numbers, and I'd like to summarize the numbers that mattered most to my dad:

- ○ 200 billion galaxies in the universe 8 billion people in the world
- ○ 16 million Jews
- ○ Dad had a couple hundred publications A strong h-index
- ○ Thousands of students Dad planted 20,000 trees He ate about 98,000 meals
- ○ He had over 3.74 billion heartbeats He took thousands of pictures

There are more numbers that matter:

- ○ 66 years of marriage to Sylvia
- ○ 4 kids—Unsung heroes—5 spouses—thought so highly of high expectations
- ○ 9 grandkids with 4 spouses
- ○ 1 bonus family member, Harrison—with only 1 fishing trip 6 great grandkids

This raises a question for me and us all: What are the numbers we care about in our lives?

If we figure out what numbers matter or don't matter, we know how to direct our attention. With this information about numbers, we know how to spend our time because life is final.

At this moment, I am reminded that I have just one Dad. My job is to keep his legacy alive.

Testimonials

Recommended Teacher Messages to Parents of Children in Primary Grades

○ Speak English when possible. If possible, speak English at home at least some of the time so that your children can become accustomed to hearing English. You can use your native language as well so that your children can continue to be bilingual. Holiday language and traditions can be learned in both languages, helping children understand and participate in school celebrations more meaningfully They can also tell classmates about their own holiday celebrations.

○ Encourage your children to make friends both in and out of your cultural group. Help them arrange play dates by calling the parents of their friends. Your children's teachers can help you with that, and you can ask them by note or email.

○ Introduce yourself to the principal and also to the president of the parent group. Explain that you would be happy to volunteer to help. This may feel difficult, but most principals and parent group presidents will appreciate it.

○ Be sure that you attend teacher-parent conferences. You will better understand teacher expectations and how you can work together with your children's teachers.

○ Encourage your children to become active in school sports and clubs. Do that as early as possible. Scout groups are especially helpful for connecting students. Chess clubs, Lego building or early arts clubs help children to be included and express themselves. Choral music groups help children to be comfortable in the English language. Early choral groups and bands build togetherness and confidence.

○ Volunteer to be a parent helper for school trips. In that way, you can meet your children's classmates and some other parent volunteers.

Teacher Messages to Parents of Children in Middle Grades

○ Challenging courses begin in middle grades. Encourage your students who are achieving well to choose them. It is a good time to check out individual IQ scores of students to guide them in selecting challenging courses in their areas of strength.

○ Proceed gradually with different courses. They should not take too many challenging courses, or they might feel overwhelmed and give up on challenges.

○ Sometimes high school students can tutor middle schoolers to encourage them.

○ Middle school students may form strong bonds of respect and admiration for their teachers, who can in turn motivate and inspire them.

○ Church or religious peer groups can also inspire immigrant students to help each other. They can study for tests together and learn to not give up on challenges. Immigrants may come from a variety of religions. Be sensitive to possible differences.

○ Preparation coursework for college admission typically begins in either 7th or 8th grade. Although admission to these courses is often based on student achievement, students recognize that pre-college courses are more challenging. When parents of believe their children aren't qualified or don't expect them to attend college, those students are less likely to enroll in pre-college middle school courses. Their immigrant parents don't have the middle school experiences to guide them. Without teacher guidance, capable students often miss out on opportunities to take courses that lead to college. It's essential for teachers to communicate both to parents and students when they notice high-potential learners avoiding pre-college middle school classes. Sharing observations of a student's strong intellectual abilities can help build confidence and prevent students from opting out due to self-doubt.

Teacher and Counselor Advice for High School Students

○ Educators must be especially careful not to underestimate the potential of immigrant students. While students whose parents are already professionals may receive appropriate academic guidance at home, other parents—though highly intelligent—may be undereducated and lack the experience to effectively support their children's educational paths. They may not have the financial ability to pay for college or the understanding of scholarship availability.

○ High school guidance counselors should be actively involved with students beginning in their freshman year to help ensure careful course planning that supports their potential path to college.

○ Teachers and counselors should actively encourage students to participate in extracurricular activities, especially since some may lack the confidence to get involved on their own.

○ Gradual explanation for potential college enrollment should begin by freshman year.

○ Part-time employment should be encouraged as a valuable opportunity for students to explore career interests and build confidence.

○ Community and church involvement can also be encouraged. It gives students opportunities for leadership and exploration of interests. Teachers must be careful not to rule out higher education for their immigrant students. Instead, they should actively seek out each student's strengths and interests to help guide their future opportunities.

○ Community colleges are an excellent beginning for those who cannot make the full leap to 4-year colleges. They should be viewed as a pathway to a higher education.

○ Teachers and counselors can use my book as an example of a student who started out with low expectations and a fear of participating in school extracurricular activities—but who ultimately overcame those barriers and found success. A counselor made a tremendous difference in her life, while her high school teachers—despite her earning top grades—had less of an impact.

Advice for Advanced High School Students for College Opportunities

○ Both teachers and counselors can alert immigrant students to college opportunities.

○ Alert students with average grades to community college enrollment combined with job opportunities.

○ Students with above average grades should be encouraged to apply for scholarships to a four-year college. State universities often have lower tuition and more scholarships available.

○ Once enrolled in college, students should explore assistantships or research opportunities with professors in their areas of interest. You can reassure high school students about their future.

○ Students should be encouraged to take courses across a variety of interest areas, as this can help them discover new or unexpected fields of study—both for choosing a major and for potential scholarship opportunities.

Letter from Educator Marissa Hatch

We have built something profoundly special at our school. I jumped at the chance to teach art in a place that housed only recent immigrants and refugees. The challenge of teaching students whose English is so rudimentary that we don't use standard English Language Learner (ELL) curriculum was one I leapt at, and it was a gamble that has rewarded me handsomely. I have seen my share of heartache and trauma in the students, yes, but I have also had the privilege of witnessing the remarkable growth that occurs.

It's in the shy crinkle in the corner of the eyes of my Afghan student as she laughs at my tears when, after knowing her for three years, I am unable to control my emotions at her artistic and scholastic growth. She came to this country having no formal education. She escaped the Taliban and entered school with no formal education, still learning how to navigate the expectations of classwork in a new country. Her first year was a time of transition, when she leaned on a small group of friends for support and laughter as she began adjusting to life in a new country. Now, she is careful in her art, working slowly and quietly, producing astonishing and carefully rendered masterpieces well above the quality of most of her class. She is bold when communicating with her very limited English what she cannot understand. I am often moved to tears in her presence. She and her long-time friend, a Rwandan girl, have formed a tight bond of rowdy teasing one another their emerging English and they aren't afraid to extend this invitation to me. It's become something of a game and always makes me laugh.

There are the three Spanish-speaking boys, all of whom are past high school age but are trying to make up for lost time-interruptions in their education that most our students experience. I fondly call them my "mijos" (my sons), and although they are no longer in my class, they make their way to my room at least once a day, to share a laugh or a piece of candy.

The list could go on forever. It's a happy place, where the cultures live together, a perfect kaleidoscope of identities. They start to pick up one another's languages, a Syrian boy often speaking to me in Spanish more than I've ever heard him speak Arabic, and he does it with a happy grin on his face. They are safe here, and they know it. They are loved at this school, and they are given opportunities they never had before, and we all know it. When they graduate, they will have the chance to work in partnership with a local university to achieve scholarships and support to continue that education. There is no limit to where their lives can take them. It's thrilling. Given that many students arrived after years in refugee camps or journeys marked by profound hardship, every step forward in this country feels all the more meaningful.

Truly, it's the immigrants who make America great, and it always has been, as Dr. Rimm's story shows us. My own family, along with countless others, has been positively impacted by Sylvia's work. Because immigration allowed her the opportunities to match her drive, she was positioned to grow to the top of her field. Daily, I hope the same for my own students, for all newcomers to this country. These are young people who bring resilience, perspective, and a drive to create a better world. They are here to create a better America.

I am honored to be in a position to look them in the eye every single day, even if someday I am embarrassingly moved to tears by the growth they have shown, by the beauty of their existence.

It is a privilege to know these refugees, these immigrants, these children.

This is our America.

Marissa Hatch

www.ingramcontent.com/pod-product-compliance
Lightning Source LLC
Chambersburg PA
CBHW072230131225
36558CB00007B/20